GOVERNANCE AND LEADERSHIP IN AFRICA

MASON CREST
PHILADELPHIA

GOVERNANCE AND LEADERSHIP IN AFRICA

Dr. Robert I. Rotberg

MASON CREST
PHILADELPHIA

Frontispiece: African National Congress supporters at a campaign rally, Soweto, South Africa, February 1999.

Mason Crest
450 Parkway Drive, Suite D
Broomall, PA 19008
www.masoncrest.com

Printed and bound in the United States of America.

CPSIA Compliance Information: Batch #APP2013. For further information, contact Mason Crest at 1-866-MCP-Book

First printing
1 3 5 7 9 8 6 4 2

Library of Congress Cataloging-in-Publication Data

Rotberg, Robert I.
  Governance and leadership in Africa / Robert I. Rotberg.
     p. cm. — (Africa: progress and problems)
  Includes bibliographical references and index.
  ISBN 978-1-4222-2940-8 (hc)
  ISBN 978-1-4222-8885-6 (ebook)
  1. Africa—Politics and government—1960-   —Juvenile literature. 2. Political leadership—Africa—Juvenile literature.
  I. Title. II. Series: Africa, progress & problems.
  JQ1875.R682 2013
  320.96—dc23
                         2013013028

Africa: Progress and Problems series ISBN: 978-1-4222-2934-7

Table of Contents

AFRICA: PROGRESS AND PROBLEMS

THE PROMISE OF TODAY'S AFRICA

by Robert I. Rotberg

Today's Africa is a mosaic of effective democracy and desperate despotism, immense wealth and abysmal poverty, conscious modernity and mired traditionalism, bitter conflict and vast arenas of peace, and enormous promise and abiding failure. Generalizations are more difficult to apply to Africa or Africans than elsewhere. The continent, especially the sub-Saharan two-thirds of its immense landmass, presents enormous physical, political, and human variety. From snow-capped peaks to intricate patches of remaining jungle, from desolate deserts to the greatest rivers, and from the highest coastal sand dunes anywhere to teeming urban conglomerations, Africa must be appreciated from myriad perspectives. Likewise, its peoples come in every shape and size, govern themselves in several complicated manners, worship a host of indigenous and imported gods, and speak thousands of original and five or six derivative common languages. To know Africa is to know nuance and complexity.

There are 54 nation-states that belong to the African Union, 49 of which are situated within the sub-Saharan mainland or on its offshore islands. No other continent has so many countries, political divisions, or members of the General Assembly of the United Nations. No other continent encompasses so many distinctively different peoples or spans such geographical disparity. On no other continent have so many innocent civilians lost their lives in intractable civil wars—15 million since 1991 in such places as Algeria, Angola, the Congo, Côte d'Ivoire, Liberia, Sierra Leone, and Sudan. No other continent has so many disparate natural resources (from cadmium, cobalt, and copper to petroleum and zinc) and so little to show for their frenzied exploitation. No other continent has proportionally so many people subsisting (or trying to) on less than $2 a day. But then no other continent has been so beset by HIV/AIDS (30 percent of all adults in southern Africa), by tuberculosis, by malaria (prevalent almost everywhere), and by less well-known scourges such as schistosomiasis (liver fluke), several kinds of filariasis, river blindness, trachoma, and trypanosomiasis (sleeping sickness).

Africa is among the most Christian continents, but it also is home to more Muslims than the Middle East. Apostolic and Pentecostal churches are immensely powerful. So are Sufi brotherhoods. Yet traditional African religions are still influential. So is a belief in spirits and witches (even among Christians and Muslims), in faith healing and in alternative medicine. Polygamy remains popular. So does the practice of female circumcision and other long-standing cultural preferences. Africa cannot be well understood without appreciating how village life still permeates the great cities and how urban pursuits engulf villages. Africa can no longer be considered predominantly rural, agricultural, or wild; more than half of its peoples live in towns and cities.

Political leaders must cater to both worlds, old and new. They and their followers must join the globalized, Internet-

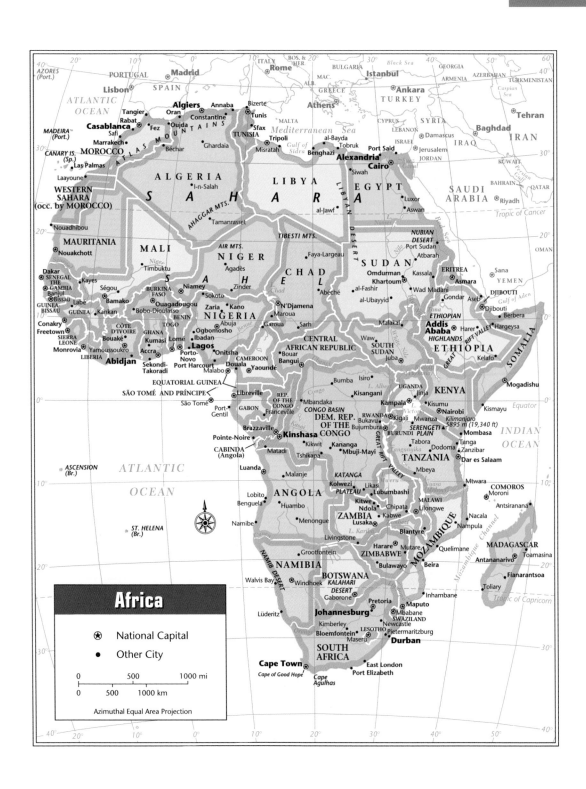

Africa

⊛ National Capital

• Other City

| 0 | 500 | 1000 mi |
| 0 | 500 | 1000 km |

Azimuthal Equal Area Projection

penetrated world even as they remain rooted appropriately in past modes of behavior, obedient to dictates of family, lineage, tribe, and ethnicity. This duality often results in democracy or at least partially participatory democracy. Equally often it develops into autocracy. Botswana and Mauritius have enduring democratic governments. In Benin, Ghana, Kenya, Lesotho, Malawi, Mali, Mozambique, Namibia, Nigeria, Senegal, South Africa, Tanzania, and Zambia fully democratic pursuits are relatively recent and not yet sustainably implanted. Algeria, Cameroon, Chad, the Central African Republic, Egypt, the Sudan, and Tunisia are authoritarian entities run by strongmen. Zimbabweans and Equatorial Guineans suffer from even more venal rule. Swazis and Moroccans are subject to the real whims of monarchs. Within even this vast sweep of political practice there are still more distinctions. The partial democracies represent a spectrum. So does the manner in which authority is wielded by kings, by generals, and by long-entrenched civilian autocrats.

The democratic countries are by and large better developed and more rapidly growing economically than those ruled by strongmen. In Africa there is an association between the pursuit of good governance and beneficial economic performance. Likewise, the natural resource wealth curse that has afflicted mineral-rich countries such as the Congo and Nigeria has had the opposite effect in well-governed places like Botswana. Nation-states open to global trade have done better than those with closed economies. So have those countries with prudent managements, sensible fiscal arrangements, and modest deficits. Overall, however, the bulk of African countries have suffered in terms of reduced economic growth from the sheer fact of being tropical, beset by disease in an enervating climate where there is an average of one trained physician to every 13,000 persons. Many lose growth prospects, too, because of the absence of navigable rivers, the paucity of ocean and river ports, barely maintained roads, and few and narrow railroads. Moreover, 15 of Africa's countries are landlocked, without comfortable access to relatively inexpensive waterborne transport. Hence, imports and exports for much of Africa are more expensive than elsewhere as they move over formidable distances. Africa is the most underdeveloped continent because of geographical and health constraints that have not yet been overcome, because of ill-considered policies, because of the sheer number of separate nation-states (a colonial legacy), and because of poor governance.

Africa's promise is immense, and far more exciting than its achievements have been since a wave of nationalism and independence in the 1960s liberated nearly every section of the continent. Thus, the next several decades of the 21st century are ones of promise for Africa. The challenges are clear: to alleviate grinding poverty and deliver greater real economic goods to larger proportions of people in each country, and across all countries; to deliver more of the benefits of good governance to more of Africa's peoples; to end the destructive killing fields that run rampant across so much of Africa; to improve educational training and health services; and to roll back the scourges of HIV/AIDS, tuberculosis, and malaria. Every challenge represents an opportunity with concerted and bountiful Western assistance to transform the lives of Africa's vulnerable and resourceful future generations.

1 MANY GOVERNMENTS, MANY STYLES OF RULE

Africa is not the globe's largest or most populous continent, but it boasts the most nation-states (54 members of the African Union, 48 of which lie south of the Sahara Desert), as well as the broadest spread of varieties of governance and leadership. Africa has its democrats and democracies, its despots and despotisms, a few kings (and no queens), some military rulers, and soldiers who have become born-again democrats.

In the bad old days of the 1970s and 1980s, Africa had a legitimate emperor and another cruel upstart who created an empire and called himself emperor. There were small-time and big-time dictators. Africa also had a number of humanist democrats who believed in a special kind of cynical pseudo-democracy called single-party rule, plus an almost never ending cycle of coup-borne officers and enlisted men who ruled episodically and erratically. The number of non-corruptible truly democratic leaders was tiny, but they themselves were giants in terms of leadership.

With the collapse of the Soviet Union and the end of the Cold War rivalries that had supported African leaders as clients of both the West and the East, a wind of democratization blew strongly in sub-Saharan Africa. Nearly two decades later, Africa is much more participatory. But still only men rule, with the lone exception of Liberian president Ellen Johnson-Sirleaf. There are fewer dangerous tyrants, more gifted participatory leaders, a widespread appreciation of democratic values, a greater flourishing of civil society, and a fuller understanding within and outside Africa that the economic, social, and political growth of Africa's peoples depends almost entirely on strengthened governance and high-quality leadership.

Sub-Saharan Africa is fed up with misrule by autocrats. In a few countries, such as Zimbabwe, disgruntled citizens suffer so much deprivation that they vote with their feet and flee in vast numbers into neighboring countries. Others, such as the inhabitants of the Democratic Republic of the Congo, stay and become inured to hardship. In some countries bad governance has bred insurrection. The African Christian peoples of southern Sudan, for example, waged a 22-year war against their Arab Muslim overlords in northern Sudan before finally gaining independence in 2011. Somali clans overthrew their repressive military ruler in 1991—and then went on completely to destroy their nation-state.

Where there is raw conflict, and the loss of millions of lives (as in the Sudan, the Congo, Liberia, and Sierra Leone), the absence of good governance and the want of positive leadership are primary causes. Likewise, nation-state failure (as in the Sudan, the Congo, Burundi, Côte d'Ivoire, and Liberia) or total collapse (as in Somalia) is the work of abysmal leadership. Even the prevalence of poverty, which reflects scarcities of economic opportunity and natural resources, is exacerbated by management error or leadership malfeasance. Leaders sometimes loot, and encourage rampant corruption by action or inaction.

THE VARIETIES OF AFRICAN GOVERNMENT

Despite such discouraging beginnings, sub-Saharan Africa in the 21st century is becoming increasingly well led and democratic. The foremost examples of this trend are Botswana, well and strongly guided in a democratic manner since independence in 1966; Mauritius, equally democratic and positively led, but also assertively plural, since its independence in 1968; and the relatively newer democracies of Cape Verde, Ghana, Kenya, Mozambique, Senegal, and South Africa.

Salva Kiir Mayardit (in black hat), first vice president of Sudan, casts his ballot in Juba during the South's historic referendum on self-determination. Sudan suffered through many years of civil war and authoritarian rule before the South voted for independence in January 2011. When the country officially became independent on July 9, 2011, Kiir became the president of South Sudan.

Another group of mostly democratic sub-Saharan African countries includes Benin, Burkina Faso, the Comoros, Djibouti, The Gambia, Madagascar, Mali, Malawi, Namibia, Niger, Sao Tome and Principe, the Seychelles, Tanzania, and Zambia. Each struggles in its own way to balance 20th-century traditions of strongman rule with new demands for greater popular participation. Democratic institutions are growing stronger in the nation-states of this category, but many of their leaders still try to exercise a preponderance of executive authority and take most decisions on their own.

Occupying a place all its own is Nigeria, sub-Saharan Africa's most populous and potentially wealthiest nation-state. Having recovered from decades of irresponsible and vicious authoritarian rule by officers, it has now experienced four mostly free (if not wholly fair) elections and is a democratic state despite many unresolved issues of corruption, resource distribution, human rights, and real popular participation.

A fourth collection of sub-Saharan African states combines a mixture of strong (but not necessarily democratic) leadership with mostly Western-oriented market policies. Examples include Gabon under Omar Bongo (1967-2009) and his son Ali (2009-present), and Uganda under president Yoweri Museveni. The Republic of Congo, under Denis Sassou-Nguesso, belongs in this group, together with Togo, now ruled after a disputed election by Fauré Gnassingbé, son of the late dictator. So does Ethiopia, sub-Saharan Africa's second most populous state, and Rwanda, under President Paul Kagame.

The two monarchies, Lesotho and Swaziland, are very different. The first now has a well-run democratic government, headed by a prime minister under a constitutionally constrained king. The second is ruled by a young but old-fashioned type of king, and the freedoms common in most other African states are unknown or repressed in Swaziland.

A sixth variety of sub-Saharan African states consists of the recovering and struggling failed states—such as Burundi, Côte d'Ivoire, Guinea-Bissau, the Democratic Republic of the Congo, Liberia, and Sierra Leone—where rudiments of participation and mechanisms for the exercise of popular choice are in place, but where those arrangements are still tentative, uncertain, or vaguely exercised.

Seventh are the dictatorships and despotisms, some even elected: Angola, Cameroon, the Central African Republic, Chad, Equatorial Guinea, Eritrea, Guinea, Mauritania, the Sudan, and Zimbabwe.

Eighth, the collapsed country without a government, is a category of one: Somalia. Although the Federal Government of Somalia was established on August 20, 2012, the southern part of the country remains largely dominated by warlords outside of Mogadishu. In the north, there is an unrecognized but mostly democratic regime (Somaliland).

THE IMPORTANCE OF LEADERSHIP

Leadership in each of these eight types of states is much more determinative and critical than it would be in older, more established, less economically fragile nations. Given the tiny (under 1 million), small (1–2 million), modest (2–5 million), and medium (5–20 million) sizes of the majority of sub-Saharan Africa's fully fledged countries, the quality of the person at the top has been and will continue to be much more important than it would be in nations with larger pools of human resources and longer traditions of political power sharing.

Indeed, governance in sub-Saharan Africa is much more dependent upon qualities of leaders and leadership than it is in other places. Rulers have always made a major difference, being almost single-handedly responsible for running down and then driving into failure and collapse a host of 20th-century states, notably Congo/Zaire under Mobutu Sese Seko, the Central African Empire under Jean-Bédel Bokassa, Uganda under Idi Amin, Sierra Leone under Siaka Stevens, Liberia under Samuel Doe and his successors, the Sudan under Gaafar Nimeiry and Hassan al-Turabi, and Somalia under Mohamed Siad Barre. In the 21st century, Robert Mugabe visibly continues to destroy Zimbabwe in the same manner, and for many of the same reasons. Avarice, in his and the other cases, trumps responsibility to the nation and its people.

Venal, depraved, and brutal rulers have plunged a number of African countries into ruination since the mid-20th century. Seen here, in a 1968 photograph, are two of the worst: Zaire's Mobutu Sese Seko (left) and the Central African Republic's Jean-Bédel Bokassa.

Rulers have equally been responsible for taking paths that led away from one-party dominance and potential strongman rule and toward participatory governance. Deciding to follow that road was not always an easy choice, but Sir Seretse Khama, in Botswana, preferred such a route in 1966 and subsequently implanted a democratic ethos that endures in his country and provides an example for the rest of Africa.

Sir Seewoosagur Ramgoolam did the same in Mauritius, beginning in 1968. Nelson Mandela selected that direction for South Africa, under especially trying circumstances, in 1994. John Kufuor likewise opted for the revival of democracy in Ghana in 2000 after years of military dictatorship. So did Abdoulaye Wade and Mwai Kibaki, after knowing long years of opposition in not very democratic Senegal and despotically ruled Kenya, respectively. Each of these examples represents a profile in courage, and an individual's personal choice of virtue over temptation. They also represent effective responses to the emerging wills of long-subservient peoples.

Sub-Saharan Africa has all too often vacillated between adherence to the all-powerful big man syndrome and awareness that such a course poorly served the cause of ordinary farmers, shopkeepers, bureaucrats, and businessmen. In a continent of village headmen, chiefs, and paramount chiefs, there has always been an acknowledgment of authority. Colonial rule did little to substitute mutual decision making and consensus building for traditional subservience to autocrats, though a few areas of Africa always found ways to check the power of their rulers through formal and informal means.

Nowadays, sub-Saharan Africa has entered an era when authoritarian rule is much less well accepted than it was in the previous century. Democracy is the norm—even though several countries honor the norm in the breach—and the remaining dictatorships are mostly anachronisms, throwbacks to an earlier period when big men were more common and the aspirations of middle classes for full democracy more easily ignored.

Much of Africa fully appreciates the overwhelming importance of good governance and accomplished democratic leadership. Each quality reinforces the other and makes more possible, in this modern, globalized century, the achievement of the objectives that mean so much to the peoples of Africa: national and personal economic growth and prosperity, improved living standards, greater educational opportunity, better health services, and the enjoyment of a wide range of political and social freedoms.

GOOD AND BAD GOVERNANCE

(Opposite page) Ugandan soldiers on a search-and-destroy mission against rebels of the Lord's Resistance Army (LRA). The government of Uganda, like other governments of sub-Saharan Africa, has found it difficult to discharge the foremost responsibility of the nation-state: securing its territory and maintaining order. Since the early 1990s the LRA has terrorized northern Uganda with a brutal campaign of murder, rape, and large-scale abduction of children.

What do we mean when we say that a sub-Saharan African country is well or poorly governed? When we report that country X is better governed than country Y, what do we know and how do we know it? On what basis can we justifiably categorize African nation-states according to their quality of governance?

POLITICAL GOODS

Governance is the effective provision of political goods to citizens. Of those political goods, the paramount one is security. There can be no economic growth or social elevation, and no societal strength as opposed to failure, without fundamental security. A nation-state's prime function is to secure a nation and its territory—to prevent cross-border invasions and incursions; to reduce domestic threats to, or attacks upon, the national order; to bolster human security by lowering crime rates; and to enable citizens to resolve their differences with fellow inhabitants or with the state itself without recourse to arms or physical coercion. If a nation-state merely controls its capital city, if it cannot project power to the periphery, if it does not have a monopoly on the use of force within its borders, and if it cannot repress secessionists and potential rebels, then the nation-state has failed or is verging on failure.

The delivery of other desirable political goods becomes feasible only when reasonable provisions of security are obtained. Good governance next requires a predictable, recognizable, systematized method of adjudicating disputes and regulating both the norms and the prevailing mores of the societies in question. This political good implies codes and procedures that together compose an enforceable body of law, security of property and the enforceability of contracts, an effective judicial system, and a set of norms that legitimate and validate traditional or new values embodied in what is (in shorthand) called the rule of law. Each of the world's nation-states fashions its own rule of law; the English common law and the Napoleonic systems are but two

major jurisprudential methodologies, and most national modalities of adjudicating disputes roughly follow those outlines. But there are other forms, either ethnically traditional or Sharia-like. Without some such formal or formalized body of laws, societal bonds weaken, disputes are settled by violent means rather than peaceful parleys, and commerce cannot proceed smoothly.

A third political good supplied in greater or lesser degrees in the developing world enables citizens to participate freely, openly, and fully in a democratic political process. This good encompasses essential freedoms: the right to participate in politics and compete for office; respect and support for national and provincial political institutions, legislatures, and courts; tolerance of dissent and difference; an independent media; and all of the basic civil and human rights. Fundamental accountability is provided by the

Toleration of dissent is a hallmark of democratic governance. Here, medical workers in Cape Town are protesting the South African government's health-care policies.

second and fourth of these freedoms. It comes through an independent, well-functioning judicial system, but also because of a fearless, free media. Few state failures have occurred in countries with open media—with a free press and privately run television channels and radio stations. Without such methods of criticism, political freedom and accountability shrink, rulers and ruling regimes can prey on their citizens (as they do in failing and failed states), and nation-state failure can occur without the wider world realizing the full extent of the difficulty.

A fourth critical political good and component of governance is the creation of an enabling environment permissive of, and conducive to, economic growth and prosperity at national and personal levels. This political good thus encompasses a prudently run monetary and banking system, usually guided by a central bank and lubricated by a national currency; a fiscal and institutional context within which citizens may pursue individual entrepreneurial goals, and potentially prosper; and a regulatory environment appropriate to the economic aspirations and attributes of the nation-state. Where a ruling family or clan arrogates to itself most of the available sources of economic growth, already-weak states become weaker and head toward failure. Likewise, a rapid rise in levels of corruption signals the possibility of failure. Plummeting gross domestic product (GDP) figures also are diagnostic, especially in developing countries that were relatively wealthy, like Côte d'Ivoire and Zimbabwe.

Infrastructure (the physical arteries of commerce), education, and medical treatment are other key political goods, nearly always the responsibilities of governments. The greater Horn of Africa region provides a useful comparative example. There, except for Kenya, all of the countries and areas are poor, with underdeveloped road and rail systems, creaky sea and river ports and airports, poor traditional telephone systems and limited teledensity, and low levels of Internet connectivity. Likewise, again except for

Kenya and northern Sudan, their health and educational systems are either nearly nonexistent or primitive (even by African standards). In the medical services field, for example, in 2013 there was one physician per 45,000 people in Ethiopia, one per 20,000 people in Eritrea, one per 28,500 people in Somalia, one per 7,100 people in Kenya, one per 4,400 people in Djibouti, and one per 3,600 people in Sudan. In terms of the number of hospital beds per 1,000 people, Ethiopia has 6.3, Djibouti and Kenya have 1.4, and all the others a few tenths of a bed. In terms of health-care expenditures as percentages of GDP, Djibouti ranks first at 7.2 percent, Sudan is at 6.3 percent Ethiopia has increased in recent years to 4.9 percent. Kenya is at 4.8 percent, with Eritrea bringing up the rear at 2.7 percent. It comes as no surprise, given these startlingly low health-care delivery numbers, the estimated life expectancy at birth of people in this region ranges from a high of about 63 years in Kenya, Sudan, and Eritrea to a low of 50 years in Somalia—15 to 25 years shorter than the average life expectancy in the United States and other developed countries.

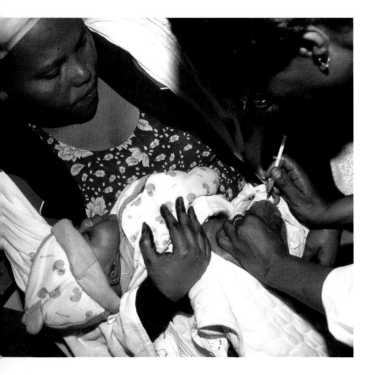

An Ethiopian baby receives a shot, Addis Ababa. Ethiopia's government has been deficient in the provision of basic medical services, an important political good: the country has just one doctor per 35,000 citizens.

What such numbers tell us is that the countries of the greater Horn of Africa region, on average, have delivered poor political goods to their citizens. Civil wars in a massive territory like the Sudan, and total collapse and the lack of most security in Somalia, plus an interstate war between Ethiopia and Eritrea, have contributed to this paucity of political goods. Few of these states have more than rudimentary rules of law. Even so, except for Somalia, these polities are secure, in some cases oppressively so. Thus, in addition to the collapsed quality of Somalia, only the Sudan (with an ongoing war in Darfur and the provision of few other political goods) is a failed state. But most of the other states of the region (bar Kenya) clearly contain the seeds of failure. The emergence of civil strife in any of them could readily transform weakness into failure.

ZIMBABWE: DESCENDING TO THE BRINK OF FAILURE

Zimbabwe represents a not untypical case in Africa where political goods, once in relatively abundant supply, were abruptly removed because of the whims of a ruler or a ruling elite. In Zimbabwe's case, President Robert Mugabe opted for the maintenance of personal power and for the personal acquisition of unbounded wealth instead of fulfilling his responsibilities as the founding father of a happy and prosperous nation.

When Africans finally created a free new nation of Zimbabwe in 1980, Mugabe became first its prime minister and then its president. He gradually gathered all of the reins of power into his own hands. Nevertheless, for much of the country's first 18 years, nearly all important political goods—security, rule of law, economic opportunity, infrastructural provisions, education, health, and the empowerment of civil society—were delivered in reasonable quantity. Mugabe indeed provided very high levels of educational opportunity, good medical services, abundant state security, low rates of crime, and excellent roads and other arteries of commerce. Corruption existed but was held in check. Economic growth was strong, based on solid macroeconomic and microeconomic fundamentals, a well-organized monetary and banking system, and a comparatively open trading system. Only freedom to campaign politically against Mugabe and the ruling Zimbabwe African National Union–Patriotic Front (ZANU-PF) was curtailed, with increasing severity. There was freedom of expression in daily life, but Mugabe's regime either owned or controlled all radio, television, and press outlets. Thus accountability was limited, even though the judicial system remained independent.

This relatively stable arrangement, with Mugabe running a strong government and increasingly intimidating or otherwise marginalizing a few brave African opponents, unraveled during the late 1990s. Mugabe started raiding the coffers of the state, permitting his relatives and associates to exceed previous levels of greed. Corruption ran rampant; citizens became increasingly cynical where previously they had been loyal and supportive. As Mugabe's legitimacy eroded, he sent 13,000 soldiers into the Congo to support another dictator. That costly maneuver bankrupted Zimbabwe. Consumer shortages of fuel and staple commodities followed. The population grew restive and rejected a referendum favored by Mugabe early in 2000.

As Mugabe became more threatened and angry, he unleashed a wave of thugs against white (and sometimes black) commercial farmers—the backbone of the national economy. When 4,000 white farmers were forced off their farms, production plummeted and 400,000 African farm workers lost their sources of employment. The national economy naturally fell backward, especially after Mugabe rigged or otherwise stole the parliamentary elections of 2000 and 2005 and the presidential poll of 2002, thus denying an emergent opposition any opportunity to put Zimbabwe back on the path of prosperity and sanity.

Zimbabwe, a strong state by African and developing world standards until 1998, has descended rapidly into weakness and to the very brink of failure. Numbers tell the story. Between 1998 and 2008, thanks to Mugabe's depredations, gross domestic product

(GDP) per capita in Zimbabwe dropped from $800 to $200, according to World Bank figures. A country that once enjoyed economic growth at a steady 5 percent a year went backwards by 40 to 50 percent during that time frame. More than 8 in 10 adult Zimbabweans are unemployed, the highest rate in the world. The local dollar, once stronger than the US dollar, steadily collapsed after 1998. Until early 2009, the Reserve Bank of Zimbabwe routinely printed money to fund the country's budget deficit, causing hyperinflation. A policy change in early 2009 that allowed currencies such as the Botswana pula, the South Africa rand, and the U.S. dollar to be used locally has helped to slow the inflation rate, but the economy is still recovering from decades of mismanagement.

In a speech following this August 2005 military parade in Harare, President Robert Mugabe (standing, right) defended Zimbabwe's 1998–2002 military intervention in the Democratic Republic of the Congo. "The timely intervention . . . by our forces," he claimed, "resulted in the creation of [an] . . . environment conducive to the development of a meaningful political process." Critics, however, noted that Mugabe and several key Zimbabwean military commanders personally profited from the intervention—while their country slid toward bankruptcy.

Equally important, by the turn of the 21st century the country's once vaunted rule of law was breaking down. Mugabe was reviling and interfering with the courts or refusing to abide by their decisions. Torture of opponents occurred. The presses of the only independent daily newspaper were bombed, and that paper was later banned. Hospitals stopped providing medicines, or even bandages. Schools lost teachers and textbooks and fell into disuse. A superbly maintained road network decayed. There were and are periodic shortages of fundamental consumer goods. Zimbabwe has experienced serious food scarcities and pockets of extreme hunger and starvation. Possibly the strongest indication of Zimbabwe's descent to the pits of governance, and near failure, however, is reflected in its alarming emigration statistics. Over the past decade at least 3 million Zimbabweans (of a nation of about 13.1 million) have fled the country for South Africa, Botswana, and Mozambique.

Zimbabwe seemed to be racing pell-mell toward failure in the mid-2000s. The state's delivery of most political goods had virtually ceased. All kinds of numbers pointed to the parlous quality of state services, and to the deep misery—a typical indication of bad governance, failure, and near failure—of the nation. However, Mugabe's regime still controlled the exercise of legitimate and illegitimate sources of violence. Although everyone was preyed upon, and Mugabe's opponents were pilloried and repressed, the state continued to project power throughout the entire country and prevent rebellion. If this situation were to change, and civil war broke out between Mugabe loyalists and regime opponents, then Zimbabwe (like so many other weak and failing states) could be called failed. In any case, contemporary Zimbabwe stands as an object lesson in how good governance can become bad governance, and how African states are so often destroyed when their quality of governance deteriorates dramatically.

GRADING GOVERNANCE

These distinctions are more than arbitrary or academic. They differentiate how important it is, and how diagnostic it can be, to distinguish in Africa (and elsewhere) among the varieties of governance. By focusing on the provision of political goods as the delivery item, it is possible objectively rather than subjectively (using the opinions of experts or even opinion polls within a country) to distinguish the good performers from the bad performers, and even to depict clearly how neighboring regimes, or regimes spread across a region or subregion, benefit their citizens.

A woman draws water near Alem Kitmama, Ethiopia. Providing basic infrastructure is a key responsibility of government.

Doing so is diagnostic. It helps outside donors appreciate even subtle differences between two candidates for assistance. But, more significantly, it supports the efforts of local civil societies when they seek to reform their own governments. Discussing governance in clear and objective terms, and according to predetermined categories of governance, also makes reform more transparent. The checklist of performance indicates which areas need to be improved the most. Such a report card might show that a country was secure but had a lamentable rule of law, or had poor educational and health achievements but abundant economic and political opportunities and freedoms.

This line of analysis presupposes that a positive goal is to attempt to help Africans realize better governance, and thus higher living standards and better services. If so, it is critical to break down the abstract term *governance* into recognizable segments (security, rule of law, and so on) and then find decent indicators of each of those deliverables so that the quantity and quality of the deliverables can be measured. When there is agreement on what is to be measured, and how to make those measurements, then it is possible to provide a report card on each sub-Saharan African country that gives grades for each indicator (each deliverable). The grades can then be summed, giving each country a score and a rank against other countries. Once that is done, it is possible to see at a glance which countries are better or more poorly governed than others and—most critically—why. If we can discover through such a method why Zambia is better governed than neighboring Malawi, we can begin to help Malawians improve their governance, or even help or shame leaders into providing more and better political goods for their citizens. That is the ultimate goal.

POSITIVE, NOT NEGATIVE, LEADERSHIP

Just as it is not helpful to talk of good governance in the abstract, likewise it is wiser to construct a firm foundation for understanding what we mean by positive leadership. There can be no good governance without good leadership. Many African examples show that leaders have usually by themselves decided whether a country enjoyed the comparative wealth and abundant happiness that almost always flow from good leadership and good governance, or the reverse. Likewise, these were decisions, not accidents, so that Africans have benefited or suffered because of the choices of their leaders.

Remember that the majority of the leaders of Africa have been foisted on their followers. Some have taken power after a military coup, and then transformed themselves into elected so-called democrats. Others have been the choices of political parties created after long political struggles and dominated by the power moves of men who either created or took over that party.

There are only a few examples of contemporary leaders rising to power purely by appealing to local electorates before running successfully for national office. Most leaders have also been professional politicians, not dentists, accountants, or lawyers forsaking an existing career because of compelling calls to serve.

In politics as in other parts of life, Africans tend to defer to seniority and to founding fathers. That is particularly so when the early leaders remain for long periods, breach constitutions that set two-term limits for presidencies, and wield the wealth and power of the state to support personal or party goals. Patronage and clientage have been significant political tools in modern Africa, much as was the case in American cities during the 19th and 20th centuries.

Yet leadership in Africa is now much more productive and performance oriented than it was in the 1970s and 1980s, when patronage, clientage, and authoritarian behavior were typical. Disfiguring examples—Idi Amin and Jean-Bédel Bokassa—were more common then. The positive role models, such as Nelson Mandela and Seretse Khama, are now the ones that Africans revere and wish to replicate. Even so, using rough-and-ready standards, during the past three decades up to 90 percent of sub-Saharan Africa's leaders have behaved despotically, governed poorly, eliminated their people's human and civil rights, initiated civil conflicts or exacerbated existing ones, decelerated per capita economic growth, and proved corrupt. Having standards for good governance and good leadership now makes it more difficult for leaders to destroy their states or the welfare of their peoples. Mugabe is the major exception; the task for Africa clearly is to build upon the positive leadership examples, and thus to alter Africa's profile of leadership.

The positive examples of African leadership stand out because of their clear-minded strength of character, their adherence to participatory democratic principles, and their rarity. In contrast, the negative examples include so many varieties—predatory kleptocrats, democratically elected and militarily installed autocrats, simpleminded looters, economic illiterates, and puffed-up posturers—that caricaturing or merely dismissing them would mislead. These single-minded, often narcissistic leaders are many and share common characteristics. They are focused on power itself, not on the uses of power for good. They are indifferent to the progress of their citizens, but anxious to receive the public's adulation. They are fre-

Idi Amin, one of Africa's most infamous leaders, seized power in a 1971 military coup. By the time he was overthrown eight years later, "the Butcher of Uganda" had ordered the killing of up to a half million of his countrymen.

quently destructive to their own countries. Unreachable by reason, they are capable of employing social or racial ideologies for political and personal purposes. They are partial to blame-shifting and hypocrisy.

DOING BETTER

A group of prominent current and former African leaders believes that Africa not only can do better, but will. In 2004, this select group decided to confront Africa's pathology of poor leadership by deeds as well as words. At the conclusion of a series of private meetings—the final one in Mombasa, Kenya—they established the African Leadership Council, promulgated a Code of African Leadership (with 23 commandments), issued a forthright declaration promoting better leadership, and proposed a series of courses to train their successors in the arts of good government. The tough-minded members of the African Leadership Council,

(continued on p. 36)

THE MOMBASA DECLARATION
20 MARCH 2004

Good leaders globally guide governments of nation-states to perform effectively for their citizens. They deliver high security for the state and the person; a functioning rule of law; education; health; and a framework conducive to economic growth. They ensure effective arteries of commerce and enshrine personal and human freedoms. They empower civil society and protect the environmental commons. Crucially, good leaders also provide their citizens with a sense of belonging to a national enterprise of which everyone can be proud. They knit rather than unravel their nations and seek to be remembered for how they have bettered the real lives of the governed rather than the fortunes of the few.

Less benevolent, even malevolent, leaders deliver far less by way of performance. Under their stewardship, roads fall into disrepair, currencies depreciate and real prices inflate, health services weaken, life expectancies slump, people go hungry, schooling standards fall, civil society becomes more beleaguered, the quest for personal and national prosperity slows, crime rates accelerate, and overall security becomes more tenuous. Corruption grows. Funds flow out of the country into hidden bank accounts. Discrimination against minorities (and occasionally majorities) becomes prevalent. Civil wars begin.

It is easy in theory and in practice to distinguish among good, less good, bad, and disappointing leaders everywhere. Positive leaders in Africa stand out because of their adherence to participatory democratic principles and their clear-minded strength of character. Transformational leaders improve the lives of their followers and make those followers proud of being a part of a new vision. Good leaders produce results, whether in terms of enhanced standards of living, basic development indicators, abundant new sources of personal opportunity, enriched schooling, skilled medical care, freedom from crime, or strengthened infrastructures. Bad and dangerous leaders tear down the social and economic fabric of the countries; they immiserate their increasingly downtrodden citizens. Despotic rulers, particularly, oppress their own fellow nationals, depriving them of liberty, prosperity, and happiness.

Africa seeks only the best and the most uplifting leadership. We recognize that leadership, especially in Africa, is difficult. There are many challenges, particularly of political culture, poverty, illiteracy, and disunity. Yet, we have come together in Mombasa (and earlier in Gaborone) to maximize and affirm the potential for positive leadership on our continent. We are not daunted by the unfortunate examples of Idi Amin, Jean-Bédel Bokassa, and Mobutu Sese Seko, and we certainly do not wish to repeat those terrible mistakes, nor to create conditions under which such bad leadership may arise or be sustained.

We assert that good leadership can flourish on the African continent. In order to strengthen the prospect of good leadership we have produced a detailed Code of African Leadership. It specifies the contours of good leadership. We want it to be the [23] commandments of leadership, and we ask the African Union, our national and continental leaders, and civil society to take note and expect each of the commandments to be fulfilled by our heads of state, heads of government, and other high-level officials.

We are also prepared individually and collectively, if requested, to assist countries and leaders to understand and live up to the letter and the spirit of the Code of African Leadership. We are prepared to help accentuate positive leadership. To that end we have formed ourselves into an African Leadership Council, with a clear mission to help translate the challenges faced by leaders into opportunities for positive performance.

We also believe strongly that future young African elected leaders should be initiated into the arts of leadership, not simply be given ministerial portfolios without the prior building of sufficient capacity. We have therefore endorsed a curriculum and a broad-based training initiative. We hope to recruit young elected leaders to attend a series of capacity building seminars regularly over the next decade.

Leadership is essential to improved governance. We firmly believe in that maxim, and trust that the peoples and leaders of Africa will welcome our efforts and support the continuing work of the Council of African Leadership.

H.E. Sir Ketumile Masire
H.E. Gen. Yakubu Gowon
H.E. Moody Awori
Hon. Peter Anyang' Nyong'o
Hon. Najib Balala
Hon. Mathews Chikaonda
Hon. Ali Khalif Galaydh
Hon. Hage Geingob
Hon. James Jonah
Hon. Abdulrahman Kinana

having codified best practices and set rigorous standards, are determined to disseminate the kind of leadership principles that will foster fairer and more effective governance in Africa.

The members of the council assert Africa's potential for leadership growth. For them, global norms are appropriate as well as attainable. Good leaders, they note, guide governments of nation-states to perform effectively for their citizens. They deliver high orders of security of the state and of the person, a functioning rule of law, education and health services of quality, and a framework conducive to economic growth. They respect personal and human freedoms, empower civil society, and protect their country's environment. Good leaders also provide their citizens with a sense of belonging to a national enterprise of which everyone can be proud. They offer a vision of what it means to be an African of a particular nation and how each inhabitant can contribute to the greater national good. Needless to say, good leaders are concerned with bettering the lives of all their citizens, rather than securing the fortunes of a few, especially members of their extended families.

By contrast, deficient (or even malign) leaders deliver far less by way of performance. They preside over deteriorating social and economic conditions. Educational standards fall. Health services are weakened and life expectancies decline. National currencies depreciate and real prices inflate while jobs vanish and hunger increases. The quest for personal and national prosperity slows, but corruption flourishes. Overall security may become more tenuous as crime rates rise. Discrimination against minorities (or occasionally majorities) becomes prevalent, and, in some cases, civil wars erupt.

Poverty within the context of resource abundance, as in oil-rich Nigeria from 1975 to 1999, indicates inadequate leadership. Despicable leadership is exemplified by Mugabe's Zimbabwe, a rich country reduced to the edge of starvation, penury, and fear.

Economic growth from a low base in the aftermath of civil war and in a context of human resource scarcity, as in contemporary Mozambique, signals effective leadership. The opening up of a long-repressed society, with attention to education and a removal of barriers to economic entrepreneurship, as in post-dictatorship Kenya, also promises progressive leadership.

THE POWER OF POSITIVE LEADERSHIP

Botswana is the paragon of leadership excellence in Africa. Long before diamonds were discovered there, the dirt-poor, colonially neglected desert protectorate demonstrated an affinity for participation, integrity, tolerance of difference and dissent, entrepreneurial initiative,

Citizens of Namibia celebrate their country's independence, March 21, 1990. In the years since, the small nation in southern Africa has enjoyed generally good governance.

and the rule of law. The relative linguistic homogeneity of Botswana probably helped (but compare Somalia). So did the tradition of chieftainship and the chiefly search for consensus after discussion among a *kgotla*, or assembly of elders. The century-old, deeply ingrained teachings of the congregational London Missionary Society mattered, too, and infected the country's dominant political culture. (But why did Christian teachings matter that much in Botswana, when the similar influence of the Protestant missionary societies in neighboring Zambia exhibited no perceptible effect?)

Botswana stands out in sub-Saharan Africa as the foremost country (along with Mauritius and South Africa) to have remained democratic in form and spirit continuously since its independence. Throughout the intervening years it has adhered strictly to the rule of law, punctiliously observed human rights and civil liberties, and vigorously attempted to enable its citizens to better their social and economic standing. A numerically small population (2.1 million) doubtless contributes to Botswana's relative success, and—since 1975—exploiting the world's richest gem diamond lodes has hardly made achieving strong results more difficult (but Angola, Equatorial Guinea, Gabon, and Nigeria all have abundant petroleum wealth, without the same striking returns for their peoples).

Any examination of Botswana, especially before 1975, shows the value of well-intentioned, clear-eyed, visionary leadership. Sir Seretse Khama, Botswana's founding president, came from a family of Bamangwato chiefs who were well regarded for their benevolence and integrity. Whatever the combination of nature and nurture, when Khama founded the Botswana Democratic Party in 1961 and led his country to independence, he already held dear those values of deliberative democracy and market economic performance that proved a recipe for his young country's political, social, and economic success. Modest, without obvious ego, not given to ostentation as a chief and leader (unlike so many of his African contemporaries), and conscious of achieving a national legacy, Sir Seretse was able to forge a participatory and law-respecting

A man of exceptional personal integrity, Seretse Khama, independent Botswana's first president, set his nation on a path to democracy and economic progress.

political culture for Botswana that has endured during the peaceful and prosperous presidencies of Sir Ketumile Masire and Festus Mogae, his successors.

In very different circumstances, Sir Seewoosagur Ramgoolam, the first leader of Mauritius, operated under the same internalized leadership codes as Sir Seretse. Ramgoolam was more explicit in charting his vision, however—much in the manner of Lee Kuan Yew of Singapore. Ramgoolam was able to give Mauritius a robust democratic beginning that has been sustained by a series of wise successors from different backgrounds and parties.

Since gaining its independence from Britain—three years after this 1965 demonstration in London—Mauritius has succeeded in creating a vibrant, prosperous democracy. Much of the credit goes to the visionary leadership of the island-nation's first prime minister, Seewoosagur Ramgoolam, and to his capable successors.

Both Khama and Ramgoolam could have emulated many of their contemporaries in establishing strong, single-man, klepto-cratic regimes. They refused to do so, in the process demonstrat-ing that positive leadership does matter. Likewise, without Nelson Mandela's inclusive leadership for good, South Africa after 1994 would have emerged more fractured and autocratic from the cauldron of apartheid. Mandela's vision insisted on vig-orous adherence to a comprehensive rule of law, a broadening of the delivery of essential services, and a slow shift away from the existing command economy toward one that was market driven.

Mandela, Khama, and Ramgoolam all led their nations demo-cratically when they could easily have aggregated personal

African National Congress leader Nelson Mandela casts his vote in South Africa's first all-race presiden-tial elections, April 26, 1994. Mandela won the historic poll in a landslide. Although he had spent 27 years as a political prisoner of South Africa's apartheid regime, as president he avoided vindictiveness toward the white minority.

power. Too few other African leaders, then and since, have followed the Mandela-Khama-Ramgoolam model. Too many have begun their presidential careers as promising democrats, only to emerge a term or two later as corrupt autocrats. Bakili Muluzi, president of Malawi from 1994 to 2004, and Daniel arap Moi, president of Kenya from 1978 to 2002, are examples, as are current leaders Robert Mugabe of Zimbabwe and Yoweri Museveni of Uganda.

Conscious that Africa's poor are getting poorer and that good governance is essential for successful economic development, the African Leadership Council sees itself as the vanguard of fundamental reform in the continent. The members of the council observe that democratic practice is mostly honored in the breach in Africa, and that mayhem is a frequent feature—witness massacres in western Darfur (in the Sudan) and in northern Uganda. Corruption still controls too many decisions, not least in Nigeria and Zimbabwe. The African Leadership Council asserts that, compared with Asia or Latin America, Africa by and large lacks positive political leadership at the highest levels.

Good leadership is crucial to Africa's growth in conditions of peace. Instead, in considerable part because of personal failures of leadership, there is conflict: the continuing civil war in Burundi, battles in the Congo, and instability in Somalia. Moreover, frequent attempts on the part of democratic presidents to breach constitutional provisions against third and fourth presidential terms testify to failed norms and deficient political cultures.

The African Leadership Council, with its Code of African Leadership and its training program, constitutes an attempt to disseminate a greater awareness of good leadership, to build upon the Mandela-Khama-Ramgoolam model, and to take charge for the first time of strengthening leadership throughout Africa. This extraordinary initiative goes far beyond the New

Partnership for Africa's Development (NEPAD) and the other programs and proposals of the African Union. The Code of African Leadership, for example, suggests that leaders in Africa exist to serve their peoples and nations, not themselves. Leaders, the code says, should "offer a coherent vision of individual

CODE OF AFRICAN LEADERSHIP
MOMBASA, 20 MARCH 2004

African leaders serve their peoples and their nations best when:

* They offer a coherent vision of individual growth and national advancement with justice and dignity for all.

* They seek to be transformational more than transactional leaders.

* They encourage broad participation of all levels of society, including all minorities and majorities, and emphasize the deliberative nature of the best democratic practices.

* They demonstrate in their professional and personal lives deep respect for the letter and the spirit of all of the provisions of the national constitution, including strictly abiding by term limits.

* They lead by example and teaching to acquaint their peoples with respect for dissent, the ideas of others, and the importance of disagreement between political parties and individuals.

* They enforce rulings of all courts and independent tribunals and emphasize and strengthen the independence of the judiciary, so as to bolster the rule of law.

* They respect international conventions and international laws.

* They promote transparency and encourage and adhere to internationally common forms of accountability.

* They recognize that they are accountable for their actions and that no one is above the law nationally and internationally.

* They accept peer review.

growth and national advancement with justice and dignity for all"—implying that most leaders nowadays do not. That is the first commandment.

Other commandments demand that African leaders encourage "broad participation," adhere to the letter and spirit of their

* They promote policies aimed at eradicating poverty and enhancing the welfare and livelihood of their people within an appropriate macroeconomic framework.

* They strengthen and improve access to education and health care.

* They respect all human rights and civil liberties.

* They demand and work for the peaceful and lawful transfer of power.

* They promote and respect the separation of powers by ensuring financial autonomy of the judiciary and parliament, and ensure that the judiciary and parliament are free from unlawful interference by the executive.

* They adhere to a strong code of ethics and demand the same from all subordinate officials and cabinet ministers.

* They do not use their office for personal gain and avoid (or declare) all conflicts of interest; they declare their personal and immediate family assets yearly.

* They specifically eschew corrupt practices and expose those in their official capacities that violate national laws and practices against corruption.

* They ensure human security.

* They respect freedom of religion.

* They respect freedom of the press and media.

* They respect freedom of assembly.

* They respect freedom of expression.

national constitutions (especially term limits), encourage dissent and disagreement, respect all human rights and civil liberties, strengthen the rule of law, promote policies that eradicate poverty and foster the well-being of their citizens, adhere to a strong code of ethics, refuse to use their offices for personal gain, oppose corruption, and bolster essential personal freedoms.

This constitutes a tall order for contemporary Africa, where autocracy is common, corruption rife, and personal aggrandizement frequent. But the bold architects of the African Leadership Council explicitly seek to avoid renewed patrimonial leadership debacles such as those presided over by Mobutu Sese Seko in Zaire, Daniel arap Moi in Kenya, Idi Amin in Uganda, and Jean-Bédel Bokassa in the Central African Empire. They are conscious, too, of the hijacking of Zimbabwe's government, resulting in starvation and drastically reduced living standards, all caused by the unprincipled actions of a president who stole elections in 2000, 2002, and 2005.

The African Leadership Council is led by Sir Ketumile Masire, former president of Botswana; General Yakubu Gowon, former head of state of Nigeria; Vice President Moody Awori of Kenya; Hage Geingob, former prime minister of Namibia; and a dozen other present and former cabinet ministers from Sierra Leone to Kenya, Malawi, and Uganda. All are esteemed throughout Africa as men of unusual personal probity. They are proponents and accomplished supporters of good governance.

The council intends to recruit additional members from among the ranks of Africa's outstanding democratic leaders. Together they will serve Africa by advising international organizations, individual countries, and donor agencies on how to improve leadership quality. Indeed, the group stands ready to assist civil societies in countries undergoing serious leadership crises. The council's members will also urge greedy national leaders to adhere to term limits (the presidents and recent presidents of Gabon, Malawi, Namibia, Uganda, and Zambia have all coveted an illegal third term) and attack corrupt practices. Together, they want to be a collective conscience for Africa.

The council further seeks to train tomorrow's elected political leaders. By so doing, it wants to instill the arts of good leadership and good governance in the next generation of Africa. Its curriculum emphasizes constitutionalism, the rule of law, ethics, accountability, the managing of diversity, principles of good fiscal management, coalition building, and the fundamentals of modern microeconomics and macroeconomics.

Whether the efforts of the privately established African Leadership Council will lead conclusively to needed reforms, reduced bloodshed, diminished corruption, and more prosperity for citizens in Africa is not certain. But, as an African response to immense needs as perceived by distinguished Africans, its innovative endeavor is rare, promising, and unique in the annals of developing-world governance.

THE AFRICAN DEMOCRACIES

African governance comes in many varieties. There are a few well-established systems with strong institutions of governance and broad acceptance of the separation of powers and the checks and balances that are the hallmark of mature or maturing democracies. Those countries follow their written constitutional mandates, support independent judiciaries, permit parliaments to check presidents or prime ministers, and prevent their executives from exercising unlimited power. There is a culture of accountability, freedom of expression and free media, and a toleration of dissent. Civil societies flourish in such surroundings. Oppositions oppose, elections are free and fair, and ruling parties are occasionally voted out of office, as in Mauritius. These kinds of political systems usually deliver the most and the best-quality political goods to their citizens.

Many of Africa's other democracies are new and still seeking to implant themselves firmly in rough soil, having replaced standard-issue autocracies, as in Ghana, Kenya, Lesotho, Madagascar, Malawi, Nigeria, and Senegal. Still others are long-established democracies, such as Namibia and Tanzania, hesitant to embrace all (or the fullest versions of) democratic norms. Where oppositions are even slightly harassed, ruling parties are given significant advantages, judges are less than independent, media are constrained or self-censorship prevails, or the regime controls most resources (especially if there is no stand-alone commercial sector), then a democracy, no matter how well intentioned, remains a work in progress. It also delivers fewer political goods, or delivers them only to selected groups of citizens.

Governing well, as noted earlier, does not depend solely on democratic values and the practice of democracy by a ruling regime. But the provision of a high order of political goods most often goes hand in hand with the pursuit of participatory methods of rule—and that amounts in effect to democracy. Being democratic means that the state welcomes the existence of opponents and lets them organize and campaign against the ruling party freely. It holds regular elections, supervised by independent electoral commissions and without finding ways to favor the party in power. It not only espouses but actually believes in and supports essential freedoms and civil liberties: freedom of expression, freedom of worship, freedom of movement, freedom of assembly, and freedom from want. It never arrests persons arbitrarily. Its trials are fair and conducted without undue delay. It gives preference to no section of the country over any other, or any group over another group. It is demonstrably fair.

The good news is that there are now many more democratic works in progress in sub-Saharan Africa than there were in previous decades. Many governments pay more than lip service to the good governance norms enumerated above. Even military rulers and despots (as will be noted in later chapters) prefer to say that they are democratic or have been "elected" to high office. But calling one's own regime democratic does not make it so. Nor is a regime democratic or "free" if it merely embraces the forms of democracy—legislative and judicial institutions and constitutions containing lofty-sounding clauses. Actions count. Adherence to prevailing global norms is essential. So is the kind of tolerance, even permissiveness, that is the hallmark of advanced democracies but that young and uncertain democracies find it difficult to demonstrate. The leaders of such democracies are often skittish—they worry about letting go and permitting the exercise of "full" democracy, fearing that special interest or ethnic groups will oust them from office.

In societies larger in scale than most of those found in Africa, government does not control so many of the paths to personal prosperity and prominence. In many African countries, being

Elections do not necessarily a democracy make. Cameroon, where this woman was photographed casting her ballot in a presidential election, is a case in point. President Paul Biya has remained in power since 1982, winning elections in 1984, 1992, and 1997 before claiming more than 70 percent of the vote in the 2004 and 2011 elections. But political expression is restricted, the government keeps tight control over the media, and independent observers have frequently leveled charges of electoral irregularities.

part of a ruling regime or close to it grants access to wealth and is the key determinant of success. For that reason, life outside of government, as an ordinary citizen, often seems unthinkable to those in power. They do not want to give up their power, their official cars and other special amenities, their wealth or access to wealth, and their acclaimed "bigness" in a small society. Such potential withdrawal symptoms are understandable, but they also make implanting enduring forms of democracy difficult or, in many cases, impossible.

Political power is more concentrated in much of Africa, too, with heads of state and heads of dominant political parties most often being the same person. Being a member of the party elite, not just joining a party, thus becomes essential to personal esteem and personal advancement. The American presidential system, with its strict central checks and balances and a legislative sector (the House of Representatives and the Senate) only loosely linked to the elected chief executive, has not been a model for more than occasional African governmental restructurings. Likewise, even a federalized Nigeria or Ethiopia is hardly as constrained as the American system is by powers belonging to the states, and by "state's rights." Most African democracies and quasi-democracies instead nominally operate along parliamentary lines, whether or not their heritage (and model) is British, French, Portuguese, Belgian, Spanish, or Italian.

FORMS OF REPRESENTATIONAL GOVERNMENT IN AFRICA

Parliamentary-type systems prevail, but only in some nations do prime ministers run their countries, with ceremonial heads of state (as in Lesotho and Ethiopia). More common are parliamentary systems with all-powerful presidents, serving both as heads of state and as heads of government. South Africa and Botswana are examples of the latter form.

Many African democracies elect their members not as individuals but as names on party tickets, again as in South Africa. The leader of the party—in South Africa's case the African National Congress (ANC), or the opposition Democratic Alliance—designates the persons on each party's slate in order of preference. If the ANC wins 66 percent of the vote in the national parliamentary election (as it did in 2009), it fills 66 percent of the 400 seats in parliament, and opposition parties fill the remaining seats in proportion to their national poll results. (In most proportional representational elections there also is a threshold of 5 or 6 percent; parties winning less than such a percentage receive no seats.) Party loyalty is thus important if an individual seeks to become politically prominent and electable. In Africa, too, loyalty to the head of the party is critical, for being allocated one of the coveted top places on any party ballot is the key to electoral success.

This form of almost pure proportional representation effectively means that there are no constituencies, and thus there is no direct representation of localities. South Africa has tried to rectify this "nationalization" of the political process by assigning members of parliament arbitrarily to constituencies—with mixed effect.

The majority of sub-Saharan African nation-states retain a constituency method of electing party members and representatives within the parliamentary system, as in Britain. This method is often called "first-past-the-post." Sometimes there is more than a single member for a constituency, but the principle is the same. In Kenya, for example, there are several members for Mombasa and many for Nairobi, while there are individual representatives for and from smaller towns like Machakos, Kericho, and Nakuru. Likewise, in Malawi, the country's three provinces are carved up into separate districts for electoral purposes, and each has a representative. In parliamentary systems, however,

Members of South Africa's opposition Democratic Alliance are sworn in at the opening of the country parliament. South Africa has a system of proportional representation whereby voters in parliamentary elections cast their ballots for a party rather than individual candidates. In 2009 the Democratic Alliance received about 17 percent of the vote, winning 67 seats in the assembly.

elected members—even though they come from local constituencies and have local supporters—face greater pressure to maintain party loyalty than do their counterparts under the American system. Members of parliaments must follow party directives even when those directives adversely affect their local supporters. Most political mechanisms are thus more centralized and centrally controlled in Africa than they are in the United States.

Although Botswana and Mauritius are Africa's most fully democratic and longest-enduring democracies, South Africa and Nigeria—because of their size, wealth, and leading positions in the sub-Saharan section of the continent—are the most significant examples of the emerging African trend toward democracy.

Their achievements, management, and organization automatically serve as role models for their neighbors and for sub-Saharan Africa as a whole. As South Africa and Nigeria go, so goes Africa politically, democratically, and—because of the tight relationship between politics and economics—economically. Winning the battle for prosperity and against poverty, and defeating HIV/AIDS and the other disease scourges of Africa, depends overwhelmingly on strengthening governance in South Africa and Nigeria. Victories in those states will inevitably lead to gains in an increasing number of the continent's less populous countries.

DEMOCRACY EMERGES IN SOUTH AFRICA

South Africa emerged from the choke hold of apartheid in 1994 when it held its first free election. Earlier, for more than 100 years, the majority of the country's inhabitants had been disenfranchised: when whites and some persons of mixed and Asian descent had gone to the polls in regular parliamentary elections, nearly all blacks had been excluded.

South Africa's emergence as a fully representative democracy followed the preparation of a very liberal constitution and the entrenching of an impressive bill of rights, after the American pattern. In order to come to terms with its troubled and contentious past, and to move forward with as much national unity and harmony as possible, South Africa also created a powerful Truth and Reconciliation Commission. The commission spent three years unearthing the gory details of the apartheid government's state-sponsored terrorism against its black citizens, granting amnesty (to a minority of those requesting it), and educating a public with incomplete knowledge about the horrors and personal devastation created by apartheid.

Since 1994, South Africa has provided a high order of political goods within a well-articulated democratic context. Despite the ANC's dominance, the Democratic Alliance and smaller opposition parties have criticized the government in and out of parliament and campaigned vigorously against it during elections. The press is free and there are many television and radio alternatives to the large government-controlled networks. A Supreme Constitutional Court, appeals courts, and provincial courts function under the liberal constitution without direct interference from the government. A high degree of accountability is provided by a critical media and a host of informal watchdog institutions, plus an open society.

In terms of political goods, South Africa has greatly extended the quantity of educational and medical services (though in some sectors with a lower level of quality). It has done well in the economic sphere, despite lower than required rates of per

Members of South Africa's Truth and Reconciliation Commission, chaired by Archbishop Desmond Tutu (center), listen to testimony from victims of apartheid-era violence, April 1996. Many observers believe that the decision to forgo retributive justice but not give blanket amnesty for official crimes was crucial in helping South Africa move past its troubled history of racial oppression.

capita growth and no reduction in unemployment levels. Political freedom and the rule of law have been broadened, and there has been a wide adherence to the fundamental provision of political goods in these spheres. The state is also very secure and projects power throughout its entire domain. However, the delivery of decent levels of human security is still noticeably absent: overall crime rates remain high, and South Africa for some time has been listed as the country with the world's second-highest murder rate.

Nelson Mandela was independent South Africa's first president. His inspired leadership proved critical both in launching a new society atop the ashes of the old and in implanting an ethos of good governance and democracy in a land that could easily have defaulted into autocracy. Despite 27 years in prison, Mandela emerged into the dawn of South African freedom without desires for revenge, and with no bursts of recrimination. He understood that his task as South Africa's initial authentic leader was to reconcile the past and harness national energies to achieve an effective future for all South Africans.

Those goals meant persuading prominent ANC colleagues—many of whom had waged a guerrilla campaign against apartheid or served time in prison for opposing the state—to accept the give-and-take requirements of a modern political system. It also meant convincing Marxist ANC members to accept the kind of market economy system that many of them had campaigned against while in exile or in jail. Accustomed as many were to command-and-control methods, and to hierarchical authority, this enlightenment of the ANC was one of Mandela's major accomplishments. Likewise, his endorsement of a bill of rights and a freestanding Constitutional Court was critical. So was his appointment of the Truth and Reconciliation Commission and his refusal to give amnesty automatically to apartheid's oppressors. Mandela set a persuasive political tone and, by so doing, rebuilt an existing nation rather than dismantling it or causing it to crumble.

But Mandela's transcending achievement during his five years as president was to demonstrate powers of forgiveness and inclusion. By donning the jersey of a white player and celebrating the international triumph of a mostly white South African rugby team, he reached out in a popularly appealing way. By taking tea with the widow of one of his main oppressors, in a self-imposed white ghetto, he demonstrated for all to see that humanity transcends particularity—and that the new South Africa was for all peoples.

South Africa could not have moved so rapidly into the midst of democracy without Mandela's instinctive, open gift for harmony over disorder and democracy over authoritarianism.

Making the trains run on time was not Mandela's specialty. He gave general guidance but left it to Thabo Mbeki, his much younger deputy president, to organize the government and deal with questions of governance. When Mbeki became president in 1999, anointed by Mandela and by the ANC, he showed that he was more interested in action than in symbols. If Mandela had not set South Africa firmly on a good governance path, it is possible that Mbeki's centralizing tendencies would have unraveled the concord between classes and colors that Mandela had forged during his presidency.

Under Mbeki, the size of the presidential office mushroomed. Mbeki turned provincial leaders as well as cabinet officials into his appointees and acolytes. He also rarely answered questions in parliament (the hallmark of the prime ministerial system but less essential in a presidential-parliamentary hybrid), tolerated criticism from the press and from the business sector less well than Mandela, and derided the opposition (especially the white-led Democratic Alliance) in a snarling manner.

Mbeki led his nation and southern Africa more idiosyncratically and stubbornly than Mandela did or would have done. He refused for a long time to accept that HIV/AIDS is a sexually transmitted disease, which slowed South Africa's response to the disease's rapid spread across the country and the continent, and left many, especially women and children, untreated for far too long. He refused to speak out against or otherwise to moderate the terrible destruction wreaked on the people of Zimbabwe, and democracy in Africa, by President Robert Mugabe. Mbeki instead saw both HIV/AIDS and Zimbabwe through the kind of racial lens that Mandela would never have used, and that Mandela publicly repudiated.

These policy lapses were also governance lapses, but they were compounded—even after the ANC and Mbeki were overwhelmingly reelected in the 2004 elections—by omissions and commissions on the home front. Corruption flourished, especially in some of the provincial administrations but also in and around the deputy presidency, in a large arms purchase arrange-

South Africa's leaders since 1999—Thabo Mbeki (top), who served until 2009, and Jacob Zuma, who succeeded Mbeki that year—have not lived up to the lofty standard of governance established by Nelson Mandela.

ment for the South African Defense Force, in parliament, and even in the transfer of shares in state-owned corporations to members of the ANC. High-handedness and intolerance of dissent also thrived.

Yet, those lapses went together with improved macroeconomic performance, low inflation rates, a tightly run fiscal apparatus, a strengthening of the industrial system, an upgraded civil service, and great strides in the shifting of economic control away from exclusively white hands. The last achievement was accomplished by creating a new black elite and enriching an entire echelon of new African entrepreneurs. Mbeki and his team compelled white-owned corporations not only to engage in affirmative action within their operations, but also to hive off portions of their firms to black Africans. Little of this trickled down to the masses, however, and "black empowerment" was a bonanza for the well placed or the already rich more than it created jobs or the hope of prosperity for the majority of black South Africans. When a large British bank purchased a major South African bank in 2005—with government approval and celebration—several key previously "empowered" Africans profited greatly.

South Africa constitutes the engine of progress for southern Africa, if not for all of sub-Saharan Africa. Its trade with the rest of Africa and the investment by South African companies in the rest of Africa has doubled since 1993. Mbeki also became involved in foreign policy, resolving conflicts in Burundi, Côte d'Ivoire, and the Democratic Republic of the Congo as well as launching the New Partnership for Africa's Development (NEPAD) and romancing the big powers of the world to devote more attention and funding to Africa.

Nevertheless, in terms of advancing good governance and democracy at home and abroad, Mbeki, along with his successor Jacob Zuma, have dissipated Mandela's great cache of goodwill. Their involvement in corruption scandals, along with their failure to condemn the abuses of the Mugabe regime, have not consolidated democracy or furthered good governance elsewhere on the continent. But it is at home, in South Africa, that many opportunities have been missed to maintain the lofty standards and high tone set by Mandela. These results illustrate the conclusion that if good governance structures are continually diminished, and the institutions of democracy are ignored or bypassed, then the spread of freedom and democracy in Africa will falter.

NIGERIA: PROBLEMS AND POTENTIAL

Nigeria should be so fortunate as to have South Africa's problems or its cohesion as a nation. A string of military dictators from 1975 to 1999, especially General Sani Abacha (1993–1998), destroyed what little semblance of nationhood or democratic practice the massive country possessed. They looted its enormous petroleum resources and wealth, transformed Nigeria from a food producer into a food importer, and turned ethnic group against ethnic group, Muslim against Christian, and northerner against southerner. All Nigerians scrambled to survive.

When Olusegun Obasanjo, a reformed military man himself, became president in 1999, and was reelected in 2003, he and his associates faced an almost impossible task. Setting an embittered collection of peoples numbering as many as 130 million back to work within a hastily constructed democratic apparatus of good governance proved a daunting and per-

General Sani Abacha reviews Nigerian troops in Abuja, 1996. As military dictator Abacha presided over rampant human rights abuses and plundered Nigeria's treasury.

ilous ordeal. Indeed, Obasanjo inherited a governance machine that delivered hardly any political goods to citizens and was believed by most Nigerians to favor northern Muslims over Christian and traditional southerners. Political unity and political will were lacking, at the top and at other levels, and the whole governmental and national culture was suffused with corruption. Ordinary Nigerians were rightfully suspicious of office-holders, "big men," soldiers, and anything that reminded them of their desperate days before 1999.

Given the abundant ability of Nigeria's citizens, the number of its university graduates, the sheer size of its middle class, the celebrated entrepreneurial abilities of Nigerians at home and abroad, and the country's leaders' oft-expressed determination to create a better nation, good governance should be achievable. Yet, good governance begins with good performance, with delivering political goods: personal security and freedom from depredation; a predictable, recognizable, systematized method of adjudicating disputes and regulating the norms and mores of a society (an effective rule of law); the essential political freedoms to participate in political life and express dissent openly; medical and health care; schools and educational instruction; roads, railways, ports, and harbors (the physical infrastructure of commerce); a functional money and banking system; a fiscal and institutional context within which citizens can pursue personal entrepreneurial goals and potentially prosper; a vibrant civil society; and a sharing of the environmental commons.

Nigeria, as a federal nation-state and as a collection of national and subordinate governments, by these criteria performs poorly as compared with other nation-states in Africa and in the developing world. The supply of political goods in Nigeria is deficient, inhibited by political disorganization; political fragmentation; religious, linguistic, ethnic, and other antagonisms; and problems of inconsistent and non-visionary leadership. It is precisely these prevailing deficiencies—especially the failure of the Nigerian government to channel Muslim fundamentalism acceptably and to make the nation fully secure—that makes Nigeria a threat to itself, to its neighbors, and to world order.

Nigeria is a centralized federation with 36 weak multi-ethnic states together serving three regions and dozens of prominent peoples who display distinct and often conflicting interests. Creating a Nigerian "nation" remains a challenge. Moreover, reconciling the strikingly different personal and group objectives of traditional northern Muslim-dominated emirates and achievement-oriented Christian communities in the south embodies a complex, continuing mosaic of excruciatingly difficult political choices. The existing Nigerian governing system—with a nominally strong executive and central revenue capture and control, the overhang of a suspicious army and numerous military and former military power-brokers, weak law and order institutions, a battered bureaucracy, macroeconomic disarray, and rampant corruption—lacks the legitimacy to navigate those choices. The absence of a cohesive democratic political culture is certainly a hindrance. Nor do a predominant lack of national vision, weak consensual political and corporate leadership, and fragile ethical underpinnings help. Sectarian violence is always around the next political corner.

A Muslim woman walks past the burned-out shell of a Christian church in the northern Nigerian city of Kaduna, which was convulsed by days of rioting and sectarian violence in November 2002. The unrest, triggered by a newspaper article that Muslims believed insulted the prophet Muhammad, underscored the volatile nature of Muslim-Christian relations in Nigeria.

Nigerian president Goodluck Jonathan speaks to the United Nations. With its multitude of competing ethnic groups, simmering religious tensions, and entrenched corruption, Nigeria is an extremely difficult country to govern. But to a certain extent prospects for improved economic and political conditions throughout sub-Saharan Africa hinge on the success of this giant, resource-rich nation.

Nigeria's governance also has numerous positive attributes: Its press is largely free and vociferous. The courts function, albeit not as well as they might. The legislature at the national level and in many of the states demonstrates an appropriate degree of independence from the various national and state executives. Civil society is vibrant, especially in the south.

Nevertheless, Nigeria suffers from excessive centralization, provoking constant pressures for decentralization, confederation, or partition. Better balance is needed, with more attention to the bottom tier of Nigerian government—the municipal and local authorities. (This arena is also a serious problem in South Africa.) Improved revenue-sharing formulas are also required to keep the nation from pulling apart. Nearly all of Nigeria's wealth as a nation comes from the oil-producing region in the south and east of the country, along the Gulf of Guinea. But the largest proportion of revenue flows to the central government, with too little, according to local critics, for the poor people living in the areas from which petroleum is extracted.

Obasanjo and his successors—Umaru Yar'Adua, elected in 2007, and Goodluck Jonathan, who took over as president when Yar'Adua became incapacitated by illness, and was elected to a term in his own right in 2011—have tried to build up and unite the nation so that a robust Nigeria can play its rightful role in reshaping and strengthening all of Africa. But, increasingly, ethno-linguistic rivalries have emerged and have often erupted into outright hostility over land, jobs, or commerce. One group always claimed to be the original group in an area or town and,

A street scene from Port Harcourt, in the heart of Nigeria's oil-producing Niger Delta region. Nigeria is among the world's largest producers of petroleum, yet an estimated 6 in 10 of its people live below the local poverty line.

spurred by competition or imagined competition, sought to oust or marginalize supposed newcomers or foreigners. Nigeria under democratic rule found that each new claim led to newer claims and, too often, to the kinds of agitation, human rights abuses, and warfare that the state and federal governments have been unable or unwilling to contain.

Nigeria is a sprawling experiment in African governance. With its many layers, its many opposed peoples (350 or so), its religious as well as ethnic differences, and its complexity—and with so many state governments as well as a national government—it is hard to imagine that any leader can create a coherent whole. Yet, if Nigeria's leaders do manage to deliver a new level of political goods to the country's citizens, and dampens conflict, the rest of Africa will profit.

BOTSWANA AND MAURITIUS: MODELS OF GOOD GOVERNANCE

Botswana and Mauritius are the two firm models of excellent African governance against which all other African experiments must be judged. However, each is a small country (populations of about 2.1 million and 1.3 million, respectively), and Mauritius, an Indian Ocean island, shares few cultural or historical affinities with mainland Africa. Part of its population (27 percent) is descended from slaves shipped from Africa to the successively Dutch-, French-, and British-controlled island in the 18th and 19th centuries, but intermarriage and broad waves of assimilation have blurred direct personal or family links to Africa—or even to other Indian Ocean islands such as Madagascar, the Comoros, or the Seychelles. Mauritius belongs to Africa mostly by political choice, but its example remains influential within the African Union and African context.

Mauritius is also successfully pluralistic in a manner that has largely escaped the rest of Africa. Its Hindi-speaking majority, largely composed of persons from South India who were brought to Mauritius to work in the sugar industry during the 19th century (under British rule), is dominant, but there are Creole-speaking (African derived), Chinese-speaking, French-speaking, and other minorities among Mauritius's complex potpourri of peoples and nationalities. Non-Hindi-speakers as well as Hindi-speakers have run the country since independence. English, French, and Creole are official languages in parliament and in daily life. There are more newspapers publishing in French than in English; radio stations are multilingual.

When Sir Seewoosagur Ramgoolam led Mauritius to independence in 1968, the former British colony had suffered many bouts of racial violence, plus a devastating cyclone. Sir Seewoosagur had two options: 1) to attempt to maintain Hindu hegemony by force or by developing a mode of popular Afro-socialist single-party rule—then common among new African and Asian nation-states and members of the Non-Aligned Movement; or 2) to elaborate a democratic model, taking his and his community's chances on the gradual development of an ethos of sharing and tolerance.

Sir Seewoosagur also understood that if he chose the second option he would have to find some means of lifting all of his nation's boats on the tide of rising prosperity. The importance of sugar, the island's only source of foreign earnings and the mainstay of all employment, would have to be reduced in order to develop new opportunities for wealth and in order to shore up his risky political undertaking.

From the late 1960s onward, Mauritius, taking the second option, proceeded to craft a durable democracy capable of providing acceptable quantities and outstanding qualities of the important political goods. At the center of this bastion of African democracy is a security system that has managed to treat all Mauritians equally, despite the island's history of intergroup hostility and distrust. An even-handed and professional national

Good governance has paid dividends for the island-nation of Mauritius. Seen here is a view of the capital, Port Louis.

police force has been critical to peaceful relations and development and to the growth on the island of a large store of political capital. Mauritians believe in the good faith and good intentions of their government.

Strengthening this feeling has been a thorough respect, at all levels, for the rule of law. Without such respect, confidence in the sanctity of the contract mechanism falters, and commercial life suffers. Likewise, if citizens can have faith in the law and legal processes, they have fewer reasons to settle disputes or express grievances through violence. Mauritius—uniquely among the countries of Africa, and almost alone among large or medium-sized members of the Commonwealth of Nations—has long allowed its citizens to appeal court judgments beyond the island's supreme court to the Privy Council of the House of Lords, Britain's highest court. This clever construct keeps judges in Mauritius conscious of the incorruptibility of law, and gives civil and criminal litigants confidence in the ultimate fairness of the entire legal framework, thus assisting stability.

Mauritius also developed various methods to assure every minority a voice in politics. It did so by privileging no language over another, creating reserved seats for several minorities, educating in several languages, developing an open style of political discourse, and welcoming the accountability provided by multiple media outlets. Sir Seewoosagur and his associates and successors effectively created a nation out of a varied collection of backgrounds, colors, and intonations.

None of these positive efforts would have gone far, however, without attention to economic opportunity. Sir Seewoosagur decided that sugar, with wildly fluctuating prices, was a dead end. So he opted for an open trading system based on the development of an export processing zone and the encouragement and nurturing of a gradually better skilled workforce. Under his and his successors' guidance, and with investments from Asia, Mauritius became a major textile exporter (importing all raw materials), and it now exports wool fabrics (Mauritius has never seen a grazing sheep), cotton clothing, cut flowers, manufactured goods such as cell phones, and many other commodities. Mauritius demonstrates what a well-managed, democratic society can become—for all of its citizens—despite extreme isolation (Mauritius is 2,000 miles from anywhere significant), small size, and a multi-hued population. Good leadership was obviously crucial.

On the mainland of Africa only Botswana has had a long, settled experience with democracy and the improving provision of political goods. Leading the country toward independence from 1961, as head of the Botswana Democratic Party (BDP), and later serving as the first president of the new Botswana (from 1966 to 1980), was Sir Seretse Khama. As a distinguished leading paramount chief of the Bamangwato, the largest group within Botswana's majority Tswana population, Sir Seretse could easily have joined his neighboring independent leaders in creating a single-party state with Afro-socialist pretensions. In other words, he could have become an all-powerful autocrat.

There were personal and family reasons why Sir Seretse chose a participatory path for his country. Descended from a family of Bamangwato chiefs who were well regarded for their benevolence and integrity, he himself believed in popular rule. He had attended Fort Hare University College in South Africa, where he received his B.A. in 1944, and then Balliol College, University of Oxford, and the Inner Temple, in London, where he studied law. His studies and his marriage to a Briton in 1948 may have reinforced his family traits. Equally important, Botswana's later democratic path may have been smoothed by a comparative linguistic homogeneity, unlike much of mainland Africa. Furthermore, Botswana—more than most African lands—had a long tradition of developing consensus through democratic discussions between a chief and his constituents. This was done in the *kgotla*, the assembly of elders, where excessive authority was curbed. Also, most Tswana people and Sir Seretse's own Bamangwato community had been steeped in the virtuous ideology of the Congregational Church, especially that passed on by more than a century of missionaries, including Robert Moffat and David Livingstone.

Whatever the combination of factors that came together in the 1960s to produce one of Africa's rare early flowerings of participatory rule, diamond wealth was not essential. That came nearly a decade later, after Botswana was well established on an unswerving democratic road. Indeed, Botswana has conspicuously adhered strictly to the rule of law since 1966, simultane-

Ian Khama, current president of Botswana, is the son of former president Sir Seretse Khama. In Botswana the president is elected by members of the National Assembly. Since independence in 1965, the Botswana Democratic Party, established by Sir Seretse, has been in power.

ously observed human rights and civil liberties, and vigorously attempted to enable its citizens to better their social and economic standings.

Sir Seretse was able to forge a political culture of participation for the emergent Botswana. This system of values governing the conduct of political affairs has endured during the peaceful and prosperous presidencies of his successors Sir Ketumile Masire (1980–1998), Festus Mogae (1998–2008), and Sir Seretse's son Ian Khama (2008-present). Sir Seretse is remembered for putting a program of democracy in place gradually, and for refusing to succumb to the external political whims that inspired so many of his contemporaries, such as Afro-socialism or crypto-Marxism. Likewise, he refused instant panaceas, such as nationalizing his productive mineral industries in the disastrous manner of neighboring Zambia. Nor did he posture ineffectively against the hideous crimes of apartheid in neighboring South Africa. Sir Seretse and Sir Ketumile were instead deft and decisive in their disapproving but non-antagonistic approach to South Africa. Critically, too, Sir Seretse engineered Botswana's control of the country's newly discovered rich gem lode without frightening off or limiting investment from South Africa. He trained his own Botswanan successors and empowered them without ever overstretching the young country's human resource capacities. He took no shortcuts. He and his successors abridged no rights of citizens.

Botswana's first president set the pattern and his successors have adhered to it, thus benefiting nearly all of their citizens. Botswana ranks among the five most prosperous African countries (as measured by per capita income), and it has consistently boasted economic growth rates that are among the highest in the world. Moreover, its institutions of governance are well respected, and its people enjoy the blessings of decent rule much more than their brethren elsewhere on the continent. Even though opposition parties have never ousted the BDP from power in Botswana (unlike Mauritius, where rule has rotated among parties), the national and local elections are fair and free, opponents criticize in and out of parliament, local civil society never rails against the government for its failure to observe all human rights (as in so many other countries), the media is free, the judiciary is free, and there is a climate of national and international accountability. Botswana is not perfect, but as Africa and the developing world go, it provides a beacon of democracy and freedom. In terms of governance, Botswana ranks among the very best performers anywhere.

5 THE MIXED OR QUASI-DEMOCRACIES

Ethiopia, with 91 million citizens the most populous of the really poor and socially deprived countries of the world, held its first free election in 2005. Voters were offered a real choice; opposition parties fielded more candidates than ever. The government even permitted as many as a million opposition supporters to march on Addis Ababa, the highland capital (although later the government banned all rallies in the city). State-controlled radio broadcast reasonable political debates. There were a host of foreign observers.

Unlike so many of Africa's governments, Ethiopia also moved to decentralize its own power, carving nine regions out of the vast state, with its soaring highlands—the source of the Blue Nile—and its hot and pestilential lowlands. The new provinces recognize the country's ethnic and religious composition, giving the comfort of some autonomy to the largest of the 80 or so peoples and languages that inhabit Ethiopia. Although about half of the peoples of the country are Christian, the Coptic Ethiopian Orthodox Church, historically allied with the emperors, is less influential and commercially controlling than it once was. Muslims now make up more than half of the population, and some of the significant regional groupings, such as the Oromo of Oromia Province, have long sought to remove themselves from Addis Ababa's control. The government's reaction to these stirrings of revolt has been to grant the right of secession, and to write that permission into the country's new constitution.

The Ethiopian People's Revolutionary Democratic Front, founded by Meles Zenawi, a Christian who served as president and prime minister until his death in 2012, has tightly ruled Ethiopia since ousting the Soviet-backed Derg (led by Mengistu Haile Meriam) in 1991. In the early 2000s, it seemed that Zenawi was creating a more open and tolerant society—what could be termed an imperfect democracy. However, the Ethiopian People's

Revolutionary Democratic Front, which is overwhelmingly composed of Tigrayans from northernmost Ethiopia, enjoys vast powers of patronage. The state that it controls owns all land, so small-holders and peasants (85 percent of all Ethiopians live off the land) are beholden to the state, and thus to the ruling party. City and town dwellers likewise understand that the party is in charge, and that they distribute permits and licenses only to those who are friendly to their regime.

Common institutional safeguards, like an independent judicial system and accountability through the media, are largely lacking in this embryonic democracy. Even the newly elected legislature, which Meles nominally serves, looks to the prime minister for direction and instruction. Civil society is also mostly new and not accustomed to challenging the government.

More recently, the country's government has been criticized for moving in a more authoritarian direction. The U.S. Department of State's 2009 report on human rights stated that there are hundreds of political prisoners in Ethiopia, including the leader of the largest opposition party, Birtukan Midekssa. The report also found that basic freedoms, including freedom of the press, are often limited by the government. According to the "Democracy Index" published by the Economist Intelligence Unit in 2010, Ethiopia is an "authoritarian regime," ranking 118th out of 167 countries. This report noted that the government had cracked down on opposition political parties and media before parliamentary elections held in 2010.

During Ethiopian elections, opposition parties often have a challenging time getting votes. Their candidates sometimes have to seek out voters on foot, covering vast distances, while the ruling party supplies its candidates with well-equipped vehicles. Many rural voters are uninformed and take advice from ruling party agents who are running the polling places. Other voters, especially those in Muslim-dominated Oromia, have complained of intimidation and vote purchasing. One international non-governmental organization termed the election in that province a "hollow exercise." It claimed that the government had tortured its opponents, arrested them arbitrarily, and otherwise silenced peaceful dissent. Teachers had allegedly been compelled to spy on students, and local officials on smallholders. So-called troublemakers had been prevented from receiving public services, hospital attention, and so on.

It is natural in such a new, unsophisticated, large, and spread-out society for the ruling party and its leader, having liberated the nation from the tight-fisted Derg, to receive broad backing. After all, given the abysmal performance of governments before 1991—especially the Derg and, until 1974, the long imperial rule of Ethiopia's feudal emperors—nearly all Ethiopians have enjoyed improved governance. There are more schools, roads, and electric and water supplies. There are marginally better medical services and much more opportunity for entrepreneurial advances. In 2012, Ethiopia's gross domestic product (GDP) increased by 7 percent, following increases of 7.5 percent in 2011 and 8 percent in 2010. Even so, according to recent statistics from the United Nations, nearly 40 percent of Ethiopians live in absolute poverty (less than $1.25 a day), and 77 percent of Ethiopians live on less than $2 a day.

Overall, Ethiopia is a prime example of those many African states that are attempting to enhance levels of political participation from limited to meaningful, and that genuinely espouse many liberal virtues and believe in essential freedoms for their people, but that still find it premature or inexpedient to loosen hard-won, post-revolutionary control or diminish the prerogatives of rule. Some of these experiments in evolutionary democracy are more well intended than others. Some—Ethiopia is a good example—actually have delivered better governance to previously deprived citizens. A few of the less scrupulous have done

When Bakili Muluzi signaled his intention to run for a third term as president of Malawi, in violation of the country's constitution, there was a broad outcry. Muluzi eventually backed down, though he did manage to retain considerable influence in Malawian politics, creating tensions with his successor, Bingu wa Mutharika.

little, or have actually done more to limit than to advance the acquisition of meaningful political goods.

MIXED RESULTS IN MALAWI

Malawi, a country of about 12 million, is another good example of a mixed democratic state where the recovery from autocracy has only delivered partial political goods to its citizens. Hastings Kamuzu Banda, an elderly American-trained Presbyterian physician and self-made despot, harshly ruled this long, narrow territory astride Lake Malawi from 1964 to 1993. A new, democratically inspired elected government, headed by President Bakili Muluzi and a number of Banda's opponents, succeeded him and promised massive trickle-up political and economic growth.

Only some of that good governance was delivered, however. Media freedom, especially of the press, was restored and a large measure of accountability was created where none had existed under Banda. Parliament became boisterous, with competing factions and a ripe atmosphere of dissent. Judges regained much of their independence, even chastising the government on occasion. Security was strengthened, and the state ceased preying in any direct way on innocent civilians, as Banda's regime had done. The economic machinery of the state was refurbished and upgraded, the country's central bank gaining a large measure of independence and, for the most part, the fiscal system of the state becoming stronger. But corruption grew, especially among the country's top leaders, and that sapped economic growth and economic opportunity for other Malawians. The provision of health and educational services, harmed by the lack of available funds, sagged considerably. The arteries of commerce—roads, railways, and air services—also suffered under Muluzi's administration.

Muluzi, in the way of several African would-be autocrats, wanted to breach the country's constitution and compete for a third term as president in 2004. But opposition within Malawi, from civil society as well as elements of his own political party, was so strong that he backed off. Instead Muluzi nominated a handpicked successor, Bingu wa Mutharika, while changing the rules of his United Democratic Front (UDF) to allow him to retain control of the party and its finances as chairman. Bingu was elected president after a major battle among a host of contenders, showing the underlying vibrancy of Malawi's quasi-democracy. Muluzi's old UDF party also retained power, but with a much reduced plurality in parliament. So Bingu organized a coalition government.

A year later, to illustrate both the underlying drive for participation and the thirst for improved levels of governance among Africans and Malawians, Bingu's shaky regime continued to try to govern Malawi, despite a lack of unity among leaders and a striking lack of resources. He and Muluzi continued to snipe at each other, vying for power. Meanwhile corruption ran rampant, and ordinary citizens suffered from a lack of steady rule and determined policy. Classrooms remained crowded, with few teachers and a scarcity of textbooks. On average, one physician served 27,000 Malawians. Hospital beds were filled, mostly with HIV/AIDS patients, but for them there were few medicines and little treatment. A lack of local administrative and absorptive capacity had prevented Malawi from receiving a much-needed multimillion-dollar

A small child in the Malawian village of Zuwala cries out for food. Despite recent steps toward more democratic, responsive governance, Malawi continues to face a series of intractable problems, including a poverty rate above 50 percent, inadequate health-care and educational systems, and rampant corruption.

grant to cope with HIV/AIDS from the Global Fund to Fight AIDS, Tuberculosis, and Malaria. As a symptom, Malawi only had two hospital beds for every 1,000 citizens, many fewer than at least half of all African countries south of the Sahara. The roads were in bad repair. Unemployment remained high, over 40 percent, and growth rates low. Malawi wanted something better, but was unsure how to organize itself to attain its goals.

MALI: THE STRUGGLE TO PROVIDE POLITICAL GOODS

Mali, a large land of desert, semi-desert, and savanna surrounding the valley of the Upper Niger River, was run by military strongmen for three decades until 1991, when Colonel Amadou Toumani Touré ousted General Moussa Traore after weeks of violent street demonstrations had undermined 23 years of authoritarian rule. Touré led a transitional government and oversaw the writing of a new constitution (in 1992). But he handed power to a civilian regime and refused to run for the presidency himself. That gesture, so unexpected on a continent long plagued by military coups and artful shifts from one soldier to the next, helped give meaning to Mali's reclaiming of its very brief democratic heritage. Alpha Omar Konare, a professor of history, took the presidency after a first-ever free election and arranged an unexpected burst of participatory rule. This mild form of democracy, rare in French-speaking West Africa, persisted under Touré himself, who succeeded Konare in 2002. Elected, unusually, as an independent, he presided over a unique form of political consensus, largely uniting disparate parties and the various ethnic groups that compose Mali. Until late in his second term, Touré's government included members from nearly all of the country's many political movements.

Until 2012, the government of Mali was headed by an executive president and a prime minister; the president, in the French manner, was elected by all voters, and the prime minister was appointed by the president. The prime minister, in turn, appoints members of the Council of Ministers and allocates their responsibilities. In Mali's case, the prime minister is also responsible for most domestic policies. In particular, the prime minister has largely been in charge of dealing with Mali's restive trade union, as well as for expanding the country's paucity of schools, finding sufficient school places for students, and improving teacher training and teacher quality. The prime minister also reports to the National Assembly, which has 147 members representing a grand total of 13 political parties. Having many political parties—indeed, allowing many political parties to sit together in the same parliament—is unusual in Africa. It is much more a European practice.

Across one important dimension, Mali is much more peaceful, and much less rent by political tensions, than ever before in its short history as an independent nation-state. But the provision of political goods is faltering, and Mali's diminished delivery of governance has begun to undermine its democratic attainments. Unemployment levels soared in the 21st century, reaching 40 percent. But the larger problem in Mali, as in so many other African countries, is youthful disaffection, largely a result of the scarcity of jobs for young people. Youths have challenged Mali's security, attacking lecturers and workers on the campus of the University of Bamako and at national sporting events. They have formed gangs, hiring themselves out as militia for the various political parties.

Increasing corruption sapped Touré's ability to provide good governance. Inflation rose. GDP levels fell. Areas of pronounced hunger grew, with nearly a million Malians being pronounced vulnerable to starvation. Many Malians with in-demand skills or high education were leaving for France at the earliest opportunity.

In such circumstances of economic privation and worsening poverty, plus social unrest, it is difficult for poor African countries to sustain democracy, no matter how admirable their beginnings. As Africans often say, it is impossible to "eat democracy." That is why even a country like Mali had so much trouble delivering many of the necessary political goods, particularly those of security, economic opportunity, education, and health. Under Touré it performed well when compared to several of its neighbors, but by the mid-2000s Mali's democracy was sliding backward.

The democracy collapsed completely in 2012. In northern Mali, members of the Tuareg ethnic group began a revolution aimed at creating an independent state in the region known as Azawad. On March 22, 2012, military leaders angry at the way that Touré was managing the crisis launched a coup d'état, forcing him into hiding a month before the presidential election was scheduled. The coup leaders suspended Mali's constitution, although they promised to eventually return power to elected leaders. This event was met with international condemnation.

Dioncounda Traoré has served as interim president of Mali since April 2012.

On April 6, 2012, facing pressure from the international community, the coup leaders agreed to reinstate the constitution and hold democratic elections. Touré agreed to resign, and Dioncounda Traoré, the speaker of Mali's National Assembly, was named interim president and charged with overseeing new elections. A new transitional government was formed in August 2012.

Despite this, Mali's military still holds an unhealthy level of control over the government. Coup leader Amadou Sanogo, a captain in Mali's army, and a number of his military allies were made part of the transitional government, and in December 2012 the military arrested the interim prime minister, Cheick Modibo Diarra, at his home in Bamako. Diarra was a rival of Sanogo, and this incident was widely viewed as a second Malian coup.

BENIN: STABILITY AND ECONOMIC GROWTH

General Mathieu Kerekou was Benin's authoritarian ruler when the third wave of democracy swept over much of Africa following the end of the Cold War in the early 1990s. Urged by France, the former colonial power, to hold multiparty elections in 1991, Kerekou, a northerner, was ousted by Nicephore Soglo, a well-educated southerner. At the next national elections, Kerekou, now assisted by France and backed by illegal funds contributed by an American corporation, received more votes than Soglo.

Kerekou presided over a stable country and helped it to provide a reasonable order of political goods for most Beninois. He won a second term in elections in 2001. However, because Kerekou controlled so much patronage through the presidency

Yayi Boni was elected president of Benin in 2006, and re-elected in 2011. He is an internationally respected statesman who served as chairman of the African Union in 2012–13.

and politicians beholden to him, he was able to rule authoritatively, much as before. In that sense, as peaceful as Benin had become, by 2005 it was still only a partial democracy, with little dispersion of power away from the executive. There were always questions, too, about the real independence of the national elections authority, controlled by Kerekou followers.

Like other African rulers—such as Muluzi in Malawi, Frederick Chiluba in Zambia, and Sam Nujoma in Namibia—Kerekou contemplated breaking the national constitution and seeking a third term in 2006. By that time he had managed to diminish the stature of Soglo's party, the Renaissance du Benin, thus ending effective formal opposition to him and his policies. However, Kerekou ultimately decided not to run again. The 2006 presidential election in Benin was won by Yayi Boni, the former chairman of the West African Development Bank.

Under both Kerekou and Boni, Benin's government has kept inflation low and economic growth relatively high at about 5 percent a year. Kerekou and his team reorganized the important cotton export sector and reconstructed the country's main port of Cotonou. They improved the roads. As an indication of Benin's reputation for economic performance and good governance, it was one of the few countries in Africa selected by the United States to receive a Millennium Challenge Account grant—assistance that is tied to good governance and political, economic, and human rights performance. Benin has also worked closely with the World Bank and the International Monetary Fund (IMF) to improve access to basic education, boost literacy, ensure basic health care, create additional supplies of clean drinking water, combat HIV/AIDS and malaria, decentralize the country's administrative structure, and battle corruption.

6 DESPOTISM AND DICTATORSHIP

Venal leaders are the curse of Africa. If sub-Saharan Africa is "in a mess," to quote Julius Nyerere, Tanzania's founding president, it is a mess made by leaders. Africa has its geographical constraints, to be sure, as well as a cascade of tropical medical ills and a complex colonial legacy. But whereas broadly visionary leadership has uplifted Asians and expanded Asian human resource capabilities since the 1960s, too many African heads of state have in the same period presided over massive declines in African standards of living while carefully enriching themselves and their cronies.

A number of Africa's current and recent leaders are capable, honest, and good. But it is the kleptocratic, patrimonial leaders—like President Robert Mugabe of Zimbabwe—who give Africa a bad name, plunge its peoples into poverty and despair, and incite civil wars and bitter ethnic conflict. They are the ones largely responsible for declining GDPs, food scarcities, high rates of infant mortality, soaring budget deficits, human rights abuses, breaches of the rule of law, and the continued helot status of so many hopeful and energetic Africans, even those living in nominal democracies.

Controlling these African autocrats, many of whom win or manipulate elections and claim a democratic façade, is Africa's participatory dilemma. Ousting them without violence is even more problematic—witness the Kenyan failure to vote out President Daniel arap Moi (1992 and 1997) until 2002 and Mugabe's ability to rig the elections in his country in his favor since 2000.

The elected autocrats like Mugabe—dictators with a legal and democratic face—have built-in advantages that are hard for fledgling, even popular, opposition movements to overcome:

incumbency; state financing for official parties only; state control of television, radio, and the daily press; the partiality of security forces; an ability to use security forces to discourage opposition campaign rallies; control over voter rolls; the gerrymandering of constituencies; and ballot stuffing and counting partialities during and after elections. Most of all, ruling parties know how to intimidate voters, particularly semi-literate rural voters who have been acquainted with only a single ruling African party since independence.

PORTRAIT OF A DESPOT

Mugabe, for example, in mid-2005 showed Zimbabweans who was "boss." His police drove shanty dwellers from their urban homes and scattered roadside vendors in a concerted campaign of destruction and demolition; in all, an estimated 700,000 Zimbabweans lost their homes or livelihoods in the massive crackdown, according to a United Nations report released in late July. Though the government sought to portray its campaign as an effort to clean up Zimbabwe's slums and attack crime, critics charged that it was really designed to punish and intimidate dissenters. Because of desperate economic conditions, hungry residents of Harare, Bulawayo, and other cities had protested against the government. Mugabe evidently decided to preempt possible additional protests by forcing children, women, and men out of their homes.

Earlier, from 1999 to 2004, Mugabe sent groups of thugs onto thousands of white-owned farms to intimidate rural workers and their employers. White and black political opponents were beaten and killed. Less well publicized, but equally threatening, were government orders to rural clinics and hospitals to refuse treatment to backers of the main opposition party. Teachers suspected of supporting Mugabe's opponents were hauled from their classrooms and beaten. Several hundred rural schools were closed by the government-directed violence. Amnesty International reported that human rights violations were "being perpetrated against people solely because of their nonviolent exercise of their rights to freedom of association and assembly." It also noted Mugabe's breaches of the rule of law.

Zimbabwe's opposition was led by the Movement for Democratic Change, under union leader Morgan Tsvangirai. It began to alter the political complexion of Zimbabwe only after Mugabe single-handedly destroyed his country's economic equilibrium for the second time in three years. In 1998, after sending the Zimbabwean Defense Forces into the Democratic Republic of the Congo to protect President Laurent Kabila's predatory regime, Mugabe beat the drums of racism by starting to confiscate white-owned farms. He also granted lavish pensions to veterans of the country's 1971–1979 war. During a time when the country's business confidence index plummeted, foreign direct investment dried up, reserves of foreign currency shrank, exchange rates fell precipitously, and the first of many fuel and commodity shortages developed, Mugabe acquired more wealth by corrupt means. Meanwhile, Tsvangirai led several protest marches in Harare, the capital.

Mugabe's answer was to incite the thugs further, and to refuse to permit the police to enforce High Court injunctions against the farm invasions. "I will never, never, send the police and army to drive them out," Mugabe declared of the farm invaders. This refusal to abide by the rule of law was not new; Mugabe and his government had rarely honored judgments of the courts. The torture of two journalists in early 1999 and the thwarted attempt in 2000 to kidnap two Cuban physicians were only two authoritarian incidents among many.

The abuse of the rule of law and willful financial chaos was not good for ordinary Zimbabweans, whose already depressed standards of living fell dramatically throughout 1999 and 2000.

In a democratic society, citizens can influence the behavior of their leaders and their government. But effecting change is much harder when one person reigns supreme and instills fear among even his closest cabinet and party subordinates. In Zimbabwe, officials were intimidated against taking collective action for fear of retribution. (Former associates of Mugabe were known to suffer fatal "accidents" while driving.) Within State House, the executive office of the president, there was the Central Intelligence Organization (CIO), a shadowy apparatus run by ex-military generals whose main task was to enforce Mugabe's dictates and repress dissent by any and all means.

A vendor in Harare salvages some of his belongings from a fire set by police during President Robert Mugabe's 2005 slum clearance campaign, dubbed "Operation Restore Order." Although Mugabe insisted that the program was designed to improve conditions in Zimbabwe's poor urban areas, critics saw it as retaliation for popular opposition to his regime.

ECONOMIC MISMANAGEMENT AND MALFEASANCE

As acute as the political and social suffering of so many African populations has been under elected or non-elected despots, so their misery has been compounded unnecessarily by economic mismanagement. Zimbabwe's fall is hardly unique. Yet the Zimbabwe case, like the much earlier examples of Ghana under Kwame Nkrumah or Nigeria under a string of military presidents from the mid-1960s, is particularly vexing because Zimbabwe has always been comparatively wealthy by African standards. Unlike countries that have relied on a single primary export, such as Zambia (copper) or Botswana (diamonds), Zimbabwe has almost always fed itself and exported tobacco, maize (corn), gold, and a variety of other minerals. In good times, it had a healthy entrepreneurial tradition of manufacturing for export and, with Victoria Falls and a number of well-managed game reserves, an attractive tourist industry.

No single exemplar of failed leadership in Africa surpasses that of Mugabe, who has been prime minister or president of Zimbabwe from 1980 to the present. In the annals of man-made disasters in Africa, his has not yet equaled the inspired debacles of Mobutu Sese Seko in Zaire, Idi Amin in Uganda, and Jean-Bédel Bokassa in the Central African Empire. But those three were little-educated potentates pursuing peculiar personal visions and vendettas in countries less robust and less economically advanced than Zimbabwe. By contrast, Mugabe was trained by Jesuit missionaries in rural Zimbabwe, became a teacher, and then studied for a B.A. in English and History at the University College of Fort Hare in South Africa when it was one of the five best institutions of higher learning in sub-Saharan Africa.

After graduating from Fort Hare in 1951, Mugabe taught in Zimbabwe and then in Zambia, at a teacher training institution.

Along the way, he obtained a diploma and a bachelor's degree in education from the University of South Africa and another bachelor's degree in economics from the University of London, all by correspondence. Subsequently, Mugabe taught in a teacher training school in Takoradi, Ghana, from 1956 to 1960.

Because Mugabe is not a mere Amin or Bokassa, but well trained and capable of matching wits with many of the world's most sophisticated leaders, and because Zimbabwe is a modern state with one of the potentially better balanced economies of Africa and unquestionably one of the best-educated populations on the continent per capita, Mugabe's madcap abuse of Zimbabwe and Zimbabweans has been that much more tragic and destructive. He has been fully in charge, lording it over his

A Zimbabwean police officer orders supporters of opposition leader Morgan Tsvangirai to disperse, October 15, 2004. The protesters had gathered outside the High Court in Harare, where Tsvangirai, head of the opposition Movement for Democratic Change, was on trial for treason. Most observers considered the charge a politically motivated attempt by President Mugabe to muzzle one of his chief critics, and the High Court eventually acquitted Tsvangirai.

A long line of motorists at a gas station in Harare. Chronic fuel shortages are but one sign of the damage Robert Mugabe's misrule has inflicted on once-prosperous Zimbabwe.

political party's authoritative central committee, his country's cabinet, and its parliament.

For Zimbabwean consumers, life since December 1999 has been a succession of very long lines—for gasoline for their automobiles or diesel fuel for their tractors, for soap, for cooking oil, for kerosene to heat their homes, for bread, for milk, and for sugar. More than 80 percent of the country's urban African adults are unemployed. In an agricultural land where national self-sufficiency has been assumed except in years of dramatic drought, wheat and other staples have at times had to be imported from South Africa. Even homegrown vegetables are scarce and expensive. With foreign exchange being rationed, and the government (which imports all petroleum products through a government-owned corporation) lacking credit, urban and rural consumers have borne the brunt of the country's financial decay.

Mugabe says that helping Kabila was a simple matter of aiding a fellow southern African leader in a time of need. But Mugabe also wanted to show President Yoweri Museveni of Uganda and President Nelson Mandela of South Africa that he counted—that he was still decisive in Africa. Equally, Kabila offered Mugabe, several of his close political associates, and Zimbabwean generals potential personal enrichment through an allocation of diamond mines and cadmium tailings. In other words, although the Zimbabwean nation paid the troops, purchased the ammunition, and obtained the fuel that permitted Mugabe's men to help contain the rebels, designated individuals received rewards from Congolese mineral concessions in exchange for this friendly assistance.

SEIZING FARMS

If sending troops to the Congo was not sufficiently damaging to his country and his people, Mugabe compounded Zimbabwe's misery in 2000 by employing rent-a-thug ex-war veterans to invade a third (1,500) of the country's white-owned farms and by threatening loudly to confiscate every last one of the remaining farms without compensation. Whatever the compelling moral justification for evicting whites from farms (many of which were large agrobusinesses) that had been in non-indigenous hands for 50 to 100 years after being "purchased" from Africans in the process of European occupation, Mugabe's bullying and the filibustering invasions immediately jeopardized the employment and wages of 400,000 African farm laborers and their families, inhibited re-investment by farmers, and chilled domestic trade and banking (which has massive loans outstanding to white farmers). The giant Anglo-American Corporation froze its investment in a new platinum mine, two South African–based construction companies scaled back their operations, and a very large sugar firm suspended fresh investments, as did the Nissan automobile company. Bata Shoes reported that its retail trade had halted. Two of the nation's largest local firms warned that profits in 2000 would fall by 60 percent or more. Since the white-owned farms produced more than 50 percent of Zimbabwe's exports and foreign exchange earnings (with gold, ferrochrome, platinum, coal, nickel, and cotton accounting for another third, and manufacturing the rest), and the resulting unrest vitiated tourist earnings, Mugabe certainly drove a long stake into the heart of his country's already weakened national economy.

There is an unimpeachable case to be made that Africans were heartlessly pushed off the best lands in Zimbabwe by more

What looks like a friendly chat is anything but. ZANU-PF supporters of Robert Mugabe have invaded the farm of Keith Kirkman (right). Mugabe's program of seizing white-owned farms for redistribution to blacks—many of whom, critics charged, happened to be his political cronies—contributed greatly to plunging food production and rising hunger in Zimbabwe.

powerful whites, beginning in the 1890s but continuing well into the 1920s. These inequities were confirmed by a commission in 1930 chaired by Sir Morris Carter. It relegated Africans to the less well watered, stonier, less loamy lands of the nation. After independence, that disparity was meant to be rectified by official purchases of white-owned farms and the resettlement of truly landless African peasants. Some of that occurred, gradually, but much of the transferred farmland, especially the very best, somehow found its way into the ownership of associates of Mugabe. The recovered lands were used as patronage spoils and have continued to be so deployed during subsequent waves of purchase/confiscation. Moreover, in those cases of genuine peasant resettlement, no resources were provided for the maintenance of irrigation facilities or other equipment. Large farms, once broken up into peasant holdings, can prove inefficient and uneconomical, whatever the talents of the smallholder. Finally, to compound the problem, the government agricultural extension services collapsed for want of funds, so the smallholders have had few sources of advice.

THE STAIN OF CORRUPTION

If the farm invasions were not an electoral ploy, used often before by Mugabe, and if the president and his cronies had not been suspected by most Zimbabweans of having profited since the mid-1990s from every conceivable corrupt practice, the high-handedness of 1998 though 2000 would not have caused so much consternation among a hitherto accepting population. Mugabe, after all, was the founding leader, and he had long been accorded a traditional form of legitimacy. But citizens can suffer only so much before a leader loses his legitimacy. This happened to Mugabe because of the Congo and corruption.

Tracing trails of corruption anywhere, but particularly in the non-transparent countries of the developing world, is never easy.

Rumors are not necessarily fact, yet Mobutu Sese Seko of Zaire salted billions of ill-gotten dollars in banks and properties in Switzerland and France, President Hastings K. Banda of impoverished Malawi built 13 large palaces throughout his nation during a 30-year reign from 1964 to 1994, and Mugabe is known to have purchased or constructed six "mansions" in Zimbabwe. It is also a fact that he has on numerous occasions commandeered jet aircraft of the national airline (thus inconveniencing scheduled passengers) to fly abroad for supposed state "shopping" visits. It is reported that he has purchased property in Scotland and has shipped furniture from Zimbabwe in government-controlled aircraft to fill up his large house or houses overseas.

Major construction contracts, including those for Harare's new international airport, have found their way to consortia controlled by Leo Mugabe, the president's nephew. In 2000 friends of the president created a diamond harvesting scheme in the Congo. In 1997 Mugabe sought unsuccessfully (losing three court battles) to prevent a local indigenous entrepreneur from starting a successful cell telephone franchise; Mugabe wanted his nephew to be the dominant figure in the cell phone business. Whatever the totality and the truth of this circumstantial evidence, ordinary Zimbabweans in 1999 and 2000 simply rolled their eyes when questions arose about the president's rumored corruption. He and his administration were perceived as thoroughly corrupt. Indeed, part of the job of the CIO was to keep tabs on the corruption of subordinates so that Mugabe always had knowledge of and leverage over those who profited (and few had not) from their positions of public trust.

Zimbabwe, like so many African examples, has structural and geographical weaknesses. It is landlocked, for one, and is burdened with one of the highest HIV/AIDS adult prevalence rates in the world (27 percent). It also endured 90 years of white settler occupation and resource misallocation, as well as a bitter civil war. But its dismal failure to realize its lofty potential as a state that delivers more and more political and economic goods (better education, medical services, roads, communication facilities, and opportunities for improved living standards) to its 13.1 million people reflects the self-aggrandizement of its longtime leader. Largely unchallenged until he began to match his own personal gain with a massive national loss, Mugabe displays a disdain for his citizens that is bold, freshly arrogant, and unexpected in one so previously acute politically. As in the case of other modern African potentates, what went wrong? What changed?

THE RISE OF ROBERT MUGABE

After Ian Smith attempted to create a settler-ruled Rhodesia (1965–1979), Mugabe and other Zimbabwean nationalists were severely tested. They were jailed and exiled, and their leadership edges were honed by the determined aggression of the white settlers. Mugabe spent 10 years, from 1964 to 1974, in detention. When Zimbabweans—backed by China, Cuba, Libya, Algeria, Marxist Ethiopia, and others—took to the bush and began an eight-year (1971–1979) guerrilla war against Rhodesia, Mugabe emerged ascendant. He fled Zimbabwe in 1975 and rapidly consolidated his embryonic claim to national leadership by becoming both the political voice of the guerrilla struggle and by obtaining the funds and weapons necessary to pursue the war and make the combat costly for whites. Mugabe was never the field strategist. But he fueled the efforts of the guerrillas and refined the political message for which the guerrillas fought and died. (Joshua Nkomo had a separate set of less-successful guerrillas, backed by the Soviet Union.)

Zimbabwe, as an African-run enterprise, has been Mugabe's creation. Despite an evident awareness of the perils of state interventionism after years observing the economic problems of

Zambia and Mozambique at close hand, Mugabe created a crypto-Marxist state in Zimbabwe after 1980. Members of ZANU-PF were officially called "comrade." The ruling party was more powerful than the government. The nation's foreign policies were "non-aligned" yet pro-Soviet. He presided over the nationalization of newspapers, the national airline, and the marketing of minerals. Hindered for seven years by the British-imposed constitution, he waited until 1987 to scrap the country's inherited parliamentary system and become executive president and the state's unquestioned leader.

It was in the early 1990s that Mugabe's dictates became less and less subject to criticism and questioning. By the end of the decade, there was no independent press to utter dissent, and the cabinet and central committee were obedient; in addition, Mugabe's political party had earlier merged with, and absorbed, Joshua Nkomo's party (after Mugabe's militant quashing of opposition in southern Matabeleland, where some 20,000 to 30,000 supporters of Nkomo were killed).

As Mugabe successfully consolidated his grip on power at home and became a recognized world figure abroad, he became more autocratic and more avaricious. Those who were close to Mugabe in his government attribute their leader's increasing arrogance and vanity to his rising age (Mugabe turned 81 in 2005), his anxiety about being eclipsed as an African leader by Nelson Mandela after 1994, and the influence of the president's second wife. The upsurge in Mugabe's property purchases, overseas excursions, visible corruption, and capricious decision making is associated with her rise to prominence.

Lord Acton's "absolute power corrupts absolutely" is suggestive in the Mugabe case, but hardly conclusive. Nor does Mugabe's slide from principled guerrilla leader to corrupt despot reveal why he chose (unlike the first three presidents of neighboring Botswana) to mutate his acquired legitimacy into anti-democratic forms. In his case, as in so many others in Africa since 1960, the weaknesses of local civil society provided openings for autocracy. Cold War rivalries—and the tolerance for strongman rulers, which was a feature of the Cold War period, especially after a brutal civil conflict—offered further openings to nascent authoritarianism. African societies (but less Zimbabwe than most) traditionally respect and to some extent favor the accumulation of power in the hands of strong leaders. Zimbabwe, and many other African states during the Cold War era, lacked independent media that could hold politicians accountable. In Zimbabwe's case, the state's takeover of the daily press (it already owned radio and television) obviated the publicizing of government mistakes or misfeasance. Mugabe originally also created a socialist state where the party was dominant. Given the comparative prosperity of the 1980s, the absence of any real victimization of whites, and the repression and then the co-optation of Nkomo and his Ndebele party, opposition to Mugabe was muted.

The combination of dampened complaints and the brutal quashing of critics gave Mugabe an easy ride. The CIO kept internal ZANU-PF dissidents in line. So did the patronage machine that Mugabe, as patrimonial as Mobutu, utilized to entrench his personal rule. By the early 1990s, Mugabe was supreme, and largely unassailable. Cabinet ministers and the central committee answered to him. Sycophancy was the rule of politics. Those African politicians who did oppose Mugabe and the ZANU-PF steamroller either lacked national legitimacy, like Bishop Abel Muzorewa, or were harassed and arrested, like the Rev. Ndabaningi Sithole and Edgar Tekere. Moreover, ZANU-PF was formidable ethnically and politically. It was thus comparatively easy for someone effectively unchallenged either internally or externally to assume that ascendancy was a personal entitlement. This sense of entitlement often promotes excesses. His vision was "of the past," not the future.

Another important factor contributing to Mugabe's sense of invincibility was the forgiving attitude of the international community. No one in Africa ever publicly called Mugabe to account. Nyerere was greatly displeased when Mugabe rebuffed his plea not to send troops to the Congo. Mandela regarded him as an insufferable autocrat. It is likely that other leaders felt the same way. But none said so publicly.

Outside of Africa, the international lending institutions always sought to woo Mugabe, not criticize his excesses. Engagement was regarded as a better strategy than ostracism. Indeed, the IMF rewarded his negative behavior with balance of payments support. Even after Mugabe and his finance ministers refused over and over again to fulfill their bargains with the

A reader in Harare learns from the government-owned *Herald* newspaper that Zimbabwe has withdrawn from the Commonwealth, December 8, 2003. Earlier the association of independent states that formerly composed the British Empire had imposed sanctions on Zimbabwe because of what it considered unfair elections.

IMF—when targets were missed and conditions repeatedly unmet—the IMF continued to reward Mugabe's autocratic behavior. Even after he sent troops into the Congo, the IMF continued to back him. The World Bank and other donors never flagged in their support of Mugabe—whatever his high-handed flaunting of personal power from the later 1990s until 2002.

In March of 2008, Zimbabwe held joint presidential and parliamentary elections. The results, which took more than a month to be tallied and then recounted, again proved controversial. The Movement for Democratic Change (MDC) won a majority of seats in Parliament, and Mugabe's rival Morgan Tsvangirai won in the general election—but not by the margin dictated by Zimbabwean law to earn him the presidency. A run-off election was scheduled for June, but Tsvangirai withdrew, citing violence against his supporters and a lack of faith in the fairness of the process. Mugabe won the presidency by default, but critics within Zimbabwe and around the globe questioned the legitimacy of his victory.

The flawed elections of 2008 settled nothing and in fact caused even greater turmoil among the people of Zimbabwe. Leaders from the neighboring countries of South Africa and Mozambique stepped in and tried to negotiate. In September of 2008, their efforts led to a power-sharing agreement or "Unity Government" in which Mugabe retained his presidency but Tsvangirai was made Prime Minister in early 2009. In theory, this power-sharing agreement may create greater freedom in Zimbabwe; however, to date real change has not been apparent.

CURBING THE EXCESSES OF AFRICAN AUTOCRATS

More conditions, strictly observed, might be one recipe to curb the rise of future Mugabes. When it is obvious that a leader puts the interests of himself and his coterie ahead of his people— when there is factual evidence of a predatory predisposition—it behooves the international lending institutions to use tough love to attempt to curb excesses. That tough love ought to consist of an absolute refusal to lend and donate, the better to reinforce notions of constitutionalism, good governance, and sensible economic policy. Likewise, bilateral donors should simply cease supporting those prone to self-aggrandizement or abuse of human rights. Better yet, because it sends an important message and affects individuals as well as countries, donors and the international lending agencies should shun all dealings with those who breach their own national norms. No state visits for the Mugabes of the world. No welcoming of their foreign ministers or finance ministers. Ostracism can be a powerful weapon, especially if the refusal to pursue business as usual with dictators and illiberal democrats becomes common.

Continuing big power relations with the Mugabes of the world is usually excused by calling it constructive engagement or

Robert Mugabe (front row, second from left) mingled with African heads of state and World Bank and International Monetary Fund officials at this 2001 development conference in Dar es Salaam, Tanzania. Critics of Mugabe urge world leaders to exclude him from such events to deprive him of legitimacy.

quiet diplomacy. It is believed better to retain some influence, however limited, with despots. That is the usual rationale. But Mugabe grew more and more insufferable because he could thumb his nose at the international lending institutions, the Commonwealth, and the big powers of the world. No one called him to account. No one called his bluff.

There is a case to be made for giving positive reinforcement to good leadership in Africa. Participatory leadership should be supported. Sensible economic management should likewise be backed. But not the reverse. It is just possible that Mugabe's growth as an unlimited autocrat could have been checked by a rash of international cold shoulders. If he had been made unwelcome elsewhere, especially in Europe and the United States, Zimbabwean civil society might have taken heart. So might his critics in and out of government. At the very least, the international lending institutions ought to abide by the letter and spirit of their own conditions; better yet, they should write tougher ones. Had Mugabe's Zimbabwe been deprived of foreign aid because of the proclivities of its leader, subsequent suffering and the stress of recent years might have been avoided. Constructive engagement, in other words, ought to be employed in African situations only sparingly and surgically.

It is possible to be proactive about the leadership problem in Africa. It is now more necessary than ever to find ways to build capacity for leadership among elected African politicians—not in society at large (although that is not harmful), and not at the grassroots level (also useful but not sufficient). The models of modern Botswana and Mauritius, and the positive example capable of being derived from South Africa, need to be offered to emerging African elected leaders. Doing so would not be a conclusive remedy for African leadership weaknesses, but it might help limit the rise of future Mugabes and their ilk.

Glossary

APARTHEID—a former policy of racial segregation and political and economic discrimination against non-whites in South Africa.

AUTOCRAT—a leader who rules with unlimited power.

CIVIL SOCIETY—the totality of institutions, organizations, and groups that exist independent of the state and family and that, broadly speaking, focus on social development and the public interest. Civil society encompasses, for example, human rights advocacy groups, labor unions, charity organizations, and consumer rights and conservation groups.

COMMAND ECONOMY—an economic system in which decisions such as what goods to produce, in what quantities, and at what locations are made by government planners rather than being left to market forces.

GROSS DOMESTIC PRODUCT (GDP)—an important measure of the overall size of a country's economy, representing the total value of goods and services produced within the country in a one-year period.

GROSS DOMESTIC PRODUCT (GDP) PER CAPITA—an important measure of a country's prosperity or poverty, representing each citizen's average share of the country's economic activity (calculated by dividing GDP by population).

INTERNATIONAL MONETARY FUND (IMF)—an international organization, composed of 184 member countries, that seeks to promote monetary cooperation, economic growth, and development and that lends money to low-income nations.

KLEPTOCRAT—a leader given to looting and stealing at the public's expense.

MACROECONOMIC—relating to the large-scale functioning of an economy.

MICROECONOMIC—relating to the activities or functions of individual parts of an economy (such as a single sector).

SMALLHOLDER—a person who owns and works a small farm.

TELEDENSITY—the number of landline telephones per 100 people.

WORLD BANK—an international institution that provides loans and economic advice to developing nations.

Further Reading

Barkan, Joel D., and David Gordon. "Democracy in Africa." *Foreign Affairs* LXXVII (1998): 107–111.

Chege, Michael. "Sub-Saharan Africa: Underdevelopment's Last Stand." In Barbara Stallings (ed.), *Global Change, Regional Response: The New International Context of Development*, 309–345. New York: Cambridge University Press, 1995.

Dowden, Richard. *Africa: Altered States, Ordinary Miracles*. New York: Public Affairs, 2010.

Herbst, Jeffrey. *States and Power in Africa: Comparative Lessons in Authority and Control*. Princeton, N.J.: Princeton University Press, 2000.

Meredith, Martin. *The Fate of Africa: A History of the Continent Since Independence*. New York: Public Affairs, 2011.

Rotberg, Robert I. *Transformative Political Leadership: Making a Difference in the Developing World*. Chicago: University of Chicago Press, 2012.

———, ed. *Crafting the New Nigeria: Confronting the Challenges*. Boulder, Colo.: Lynne Rienner, 2004.

———, ed. *When States Fail: Causes and Consequences*. Princeton, N.J.: Princeton University Press, 2004.

———, ed. *State Failure and State Weakness in a Time of Terror.* Washington, D.C.: Brookings Institution Press, 2003.

———. "The Roots of Africa's Leadership Deficit." *Compass: A Journal of Leadership* I (2003): 28–32.

———. "Strengthening African Leadership." *Foreign Affairs* LXXXIII (2004): 14–18.

———. *Ending Autocracy, Enabling Democracy: The Tribulations of Southern Africa, 1960–2000.* Washington, D.C.: Brookings Institution Press, 2002.

Shillington, Kevin. *History of Africa.* New York: Palgrave Macmillan, 2012.

Widner, Jennifer. "States and Statelessness in Late Twentieth Century Africa." In *The Quest for World Order. Daedalus* CXXIV (1995): 129–153.

Internet Resources

HTTP://AFRICANELECTIONS.TRIPOD.COM/

This useful website provides election results, both recent and historical, for the sub-Saharan African countries.

HTTP://WWW.AFRICAN-GEOPOLITICS.ORG/HOME_ENGLISH.HTM

A quarterly online magazine, *African Geopolitics* contains articles on a variety of subjects related to governance, politics, development, and conflict in Africa.

HTTP://NEWS.BBC.CO.UK/1/HI/WORLD/AFRICA/COUNTRY_PROFILES/

This page contains links to the British Broadcasting Corporation's profiles of sub-Saharan African countries, with links to timelines at the bottom of the page. Each of the country pages contains a brief overview, a basic-facts section, a profile of the current leadership, and a listing of the major media.

HTTP://WWW.FREEDOMHOUSE.ORG

Freedom House is an independent watchdog organization dedicated to the expansion of freedom around the world. It rates the "progress and decline of political rights and civil liberties" in countries throughout Africa.

HTTP://WWW.HRW.ORG/EN/AFRICA

The organization Human Rights Watch provides reports on various human rights issues in Africa. Each country also has its own page on this site.

Index

Numbers in ***bold italic*** refer to captions.

Picture Credits

Contributors

PROFESSOR ROBERT I. ROTBERG currently holds the Fulbright Research Chair in Political Development at the Balsillie School of International Affairs in Waterloo, Canada. Prior to this, from 1999 to 2010 he served as director of the Program on Intrastate Conflict and Conflict Resolution at the Kennedy School, Harvard University. He is the author of a number of books and articles on Africa, including *Transformative Political Leadership: Making a Difference in the Developing World* (2012) and *"Worst of the Worst": Dealing with Repressive and Rogue Nations* (2007). Professor Rotberg is president emeritus of the World Peace Foundation.

DR. VICTOR OJAKOROTU is head of the Department of Politics and International Relations at North-West University in Mafikeng, South Africa. He earned his Ph.D. from the University of the Witwatersrand, Johannesburg, in 2007, and has published numerous articles on African politics and environmental issues. North-West University is one of the largest institutions of higher education in South Africa, with 64,000 students enrolled at three campuses.